TEST YOUR MATCH PLAY

TEST YOUR
MATCH PLAY

H. W. Kelsey

FABER AND FABER
London · Boston

First published in 1977
by Faber and Faber Limited
3 Queen Square London WC1
Reprinted 1978
Printed and bound in Great Britain by
Redwood Burn Limited
Trowbridge & Esher

ISBN 0 571 11005 3

Acknowledgements

As ever, I am beholden to Denis Young for a pains-
taking survey of my script and the correction of a
number of analytical errors.

H. W. K.

CONTENTS

INTRODUCTION

It is widely agreed that there is no truer test of bridge skill than a match between two teams of four players. Luck is largely eliminated in this type of contest, and in a match of reasonable length the better team is almost sure to come out on top. The knock-out match represents competitive bridge at its best and is for many players the most enjoyable form of the game.

This is an attempt to reproduce the thrills and spills of a tough bridge match within the covers of a book. You are invited to take the South seat and use your skill in play and defence to help your team to victory. Imagine that it is the final of an important competition such as the Gold Cup. There are sixty-four boards to play, and you will have a problem on every one of them.

As in real life, the match is played in sets of eight boards. First, the eight problems are presented on their own, giving you a chance to tackle them under match conditions with only two hands on view. A bidding sequence is given with each problem, but this is important only when it provides a clue to the opponents' holdings. If you don't like the bidding on any hand, please feel free to assume that you reached the final contract in any way that seems reasonable to you. After the set of eight problems, each board is given a two-page spread and discussed in detail. The problem is repeated for convenience, then comes the analysis and solution along with the full hand and the result from the other room. A scorecard is included at the end of each set of eight boards to enable you to keep a running score.

Although I have tried to maintain a link with reality, I have to admit that there are some aspects of this match which are not altogether true to life. In these areas I must hope, like a novelist, to induce a 'willing suspension of disbelief'. In the first place, South has all the problems. If you really had a knotty problem on every hand you would need to be sedated and carried out on a stretcher half-way through the match. And even before this your partner would be climbing the walls in frustration at not being allowed to play a hand.

Another point is that in this fictional match there are many more game and slam hands than you would normally encounter, creating the possibility of large swings on nearly every hand. This is because part-score hands do not make good problem material. The greater the strength held by the defenders, the harder it is for the analyst to take account of all possible variations in play and defence.

Scoring

For those who have not played duplicate bridge before, a few words on procedure and scoring may be helpful. You will know, I expect, that if you and your partner play the North-South cards in one room your team-mates play the East-West cards in the other. The four cards played to each trick are not mixed together as in rubber bridge. Each player keeps his cards stacked in front of him and at the end of the play replaces them in the appropriate North, South, East or West pocket in the board, which is then taken through to be played in the other room.

Since the hands are not played within the context of a rubber, each one has to be scored on its own. In addition to the trick score, 500 points are awarded for making a vulnerable game and 300 for a non-vulnerable game. The vulnerability varies from hand to hand and is clearly marked on each board. The award for a successful part-score contract is 50 points whether vulnerable or not.

Suppose that you bid to four spades, not vulnerable, and make ten tricks. You score 420 points, and if your team-mates manage to defeat the same contract by one trick in the other room they will score 50 points. That represents an aggregate gain to your team of 470 points on the board.

Aggregate scoring is used in some minor team events, but in all serious matches the difference in total points on each board is converted to international match points (i.m.p.) in accordance with the following table.

International Match Point Scale

Difference on board	i.m.p.	Difference on board	i.m.p.	Difference on board	i.m.p.
0– 10	0	370– 420	9	1750–1990	18
20– 40	1	430– 490	10	2000–2240	19
50– 80	2	500– 590	11	2250–2490	20
90–120	3	600– 740	12	2500–2740	21
130–160	4	750– 890	13	2750–2990	22
170–210	5	900–1090	14	3000–3240	23
220–260	6	1100–1290	15	3250–3490	24
270–310	7	1300–1490	16	3500 or more	25
320–360	8	1500–1740	17		

The gain of 470 points for your non-vulnerable game swing is converted through the above table to a gain of 10 i.m.p. It is the i.m.p. score, not the aggregate score, that is added up at the end of the match to determine the winners.

The effect of the international match point scale is to reduce even further the incidence of luck by lessening the impact of large swings and increasing the relative importance of part-scores. Two or three part-score swings can make up for an unlucky slam or an unexpected penalty.

Preliminaries

Teams may be made up of four, five or six players, although naturally only four play at the one time. Most captains prefer to have six players, for this enables them to rest each pair in turn during the critical later stages.

The quarter-finals, semi-finals and final of your competition are held in a luxury hotel over a weekend in May. Your team of six, having battled through seven earlier rounds, arrives at the hotel on the Thursday evening. You have no difficulty in your quarter-final match on the Friday, and you survive an early fright to win your semi-final on the Saturday. Now it is Sunday morning and only one team stands between you and the cup.

Naturally, your opponents are all good players, but they are not infallible. They will make their share of mistakes, and the same can be said of your team-mates. In order to win the match you will need to take advantage of your opponents' mistakes while keeping your own to a minimum.

You and your partner feel rested and quite fresh, since you were allowed to sit out for sixteen boards on both Friday and Saturday. It will not be the same today. As you finish breakfast the captain stops by your table to tell you he wants you to start against the most formidable enemy pair at eleven o'clock.

Good luck!

FIRST SESSION

Boards 1 to 8

PROBLEMS

Board 1

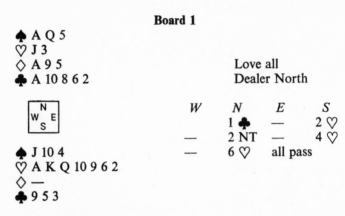

♠ A Q 5
♡ J 3
◇ A 9 5
♣ A 10 8 6 2

Love all
Dealer North

♠ J 10 4
♡ A K Q 10 9 6 2
◇ —
♣ 9 5 3

W	N	E	S
	1 ♣	—	2 ♡
—	2 NT	—	4 ♡
—	6 ♡	all pass	

The match is off to an exciting start. West leads the six of diamonds. How do you plan the play?

Solution on page 20

Board 2

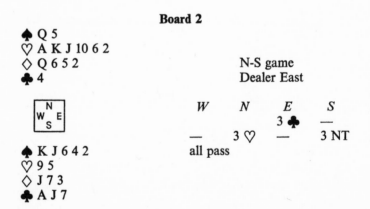

♠ Q 5
♡ A K J 10 6 2
◇ Q 6 5 2
♣ 4

N-S game
Dealer East

♠ K J 6 4 2
♡ 9 5
◇ J 7 3
♣ A J 7

W	N	E	S
		3 ♣	—
—	3 ♡	—	3 NT
all pass			

West leads the eight of clubs to the queen and ace. You play a spade to the queen and return a spade to the jack and ace, East echoing with the eight and the three. West surprises you by switching to the queen of hearts, and East follows with the seven when you play dummy's ace. Take it from there.

Solution on page 22

Board 3

E-W game
Dealer South

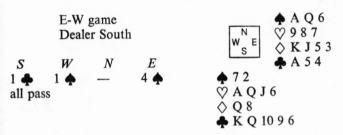

♠ A Q 6
♡ 9 8 7
◇ K J 5 3
♣ A 5 4

S	W	N	E
1♣	1♠	—	4♠
all pass			

♠ 7 2
♡ A Q J 6
◇ Q 8
♣ K Q 10 9 6

North leads the two of clubs to the ace, ten and three. Declarer ruffs a club, leads a spade to the queen, ruffs another club and leads a spade to the ace, partner following in trumps without echoing. When the nine of hearts is led you play the ace and continue with the queen. West wins with the king and returns the ten of hearts to your jack, partner following suit. What do you lead now?

Solution on page 24

Board 4

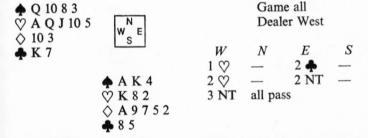

♠ Q 10 8 3
♡ A Q J 10 5
◇ 10 3
♣ K 7

Game all
Dealer West

♠ A K 4
♡ K 8 2
◇ A 9 7 5 2
♣ 8 5

W	N	E	S
1♡	—	2♣	—
2♡	—	2 NT	—
3 NT	all pass		

You lead the five of diamonds on which partner plays the king and declarer the six. North returns the eight of diamonds and you capture the jack with your ace. How should you continue?

Solution on page 26

Board 5

♠ K 8 7 3
♡ K 8 5
◇ A K Q 2
♣ 10 4

N-S game
Dealer North

```
    N
  W   E
    S
```

W	N	E	S
	1 ♠	—	2 NT
—	3 NT	Dbl	all pass

♠ 6 5 2
♡ A Q 7
◇ J 9 4
♣ A J 5 2

West dutifully leads the nine of spades and you play low from the table. East wins with the ten and switches to the two of hearts. How do you plan the play?

Solution on page 28

Board 6

E-W game
Dealer East

```
    N
  W   E
    S
```

♠ A J 10 2
♡ A Q
◇ J 4 3
♣ A 8 5 4

W	N	E	S
		1 ♣	1 ◇
3 ♡	—	4 ♡	all pass

♠ Q 7 6 3
♡ 8
◇ A K Q 10 5
♣ J 6 3

Partner leads the two of diamonds, an obvious singleton. The three is played from the table and you win the trick, with the ten. How should you continue?

Solution on page 30

Board 7

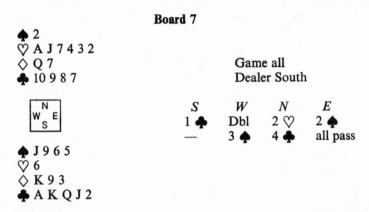

♠ 2
♡ A J 7 4 3 2
♢ Q 7
♣ 10 9 8 7

Game all
Dealer South

♠ J 9 6 5
♡ 6
♢ K 9 3
♣ A K Q J 2

S	W	N	E
1 ♣	Dbl	2 ♡	2 ♠
—	3 ♠	4 ♣	all pass

West leads the king of hearts to dummy's ace, East following with the eight. At trick two you lead a small heart and ruff high, but the prospect of establishing the suit vanishes when East discards the two of diamonds. How should you continue?

Solution on page 32

Board 8

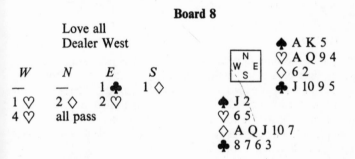

Love all
Dealer West

♠ A K 5
♡ A Q 9 4
♢ 6 2
♣ J 10 9 5

♠ J 2
♡ 6 5
♢ A Q J 10 7
♣ 8 7 6 3

W	N	E	S
—	—	1 ♣	1 ♢
1 ♡	2 ♢	2 ♡	
4 ♡	all pass		

North leads the nine of diamonds to your ace, West following with the three. How should you continue?

Solution on page 34

SOLUTIONS AND RESULTS

Board 1

PROBLEM

♠ A Q 5
♡ J 3
◇ A 9 5
♣ A 10 8 6 2

Love all
Dealer North

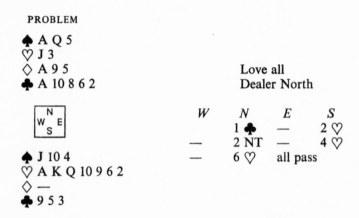

♠ J 10 4
♡ A K Q 10 9 6 2
◇ —
♣ 9 5 3

W	N	E	S
	1 ♣	—	2 ♡
—	2 NT	—	4 ♡
—	6 ♡	all pass	

West leads the six of diamonds. How do you plan the play?

SOLUTION

At first glance the slam appears to depend on the position of the king of spades, but closer inspection reveals that this is not the case. Having escaped a spade lead, you can always avoid the hazard of the finesse if the clubs are divided 3–2. The correct move at trick one is to play the nine of diamonds from dummy and discard a club from your own hand. The idea is to give up a trick to East, who cannot profitably attack spades from his side of the table.

No matter what East returns, you can cash the ace of clubs, discard your last club on the ace of diamonds, and ruff a club high. If the clubs break kindly you can re-enter dummy with the jack of hearts and ruff another club high. After drawing trumps, you will then be in a position to discard your losing spades on the established clubs.

FULL HAND

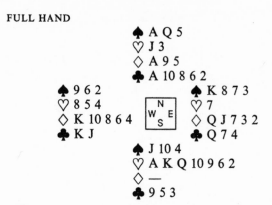

♠ A Q 5
♡ J 3
◇ A 9 5
♣ A 10 8 6 2

♠ 9 6 2   ♠ K 8 7 3
♡ 8 5 4   ♡ 7
◇ K 10 8 6 4   ◇ Q J 7 3 2
♣ K J   ♣ Q 7 4

♠ J 10 4
♡ A K Q 10 9 6 2
◇ —
♣ 9 5 3

Note that the recommended line of play risks very little. If the clubs prove to be 4–1 you can always fall back on the spade finesse.

RESULT

In the other room your opponents were less ambitious and stopped in four hearts. On a spade lead declarer made eleven tricks for a score of 450.

You pick up 11 i.m.p. if you made the slam, therefore, and you lose 11 if you went down.

Board 2

PROBLEM

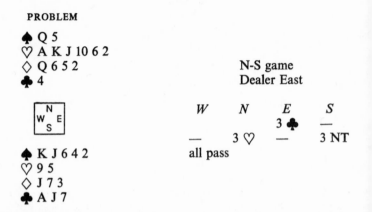

♠ Q 5
♡ A K J 10 6 2
◇ Q 6 5 2
♣ 4

N-S game
Dealer East

♠ K J 6 4 2
♡ 9 5
◇ J 7 3
♣ A J 7

W	N	E	S
		3 ♣	—
—	3 ♡	—	3 NT
all pass			

West leads the eight of clubs to the queen and ace. You play a spade to the queen and return a spade to the jack and ace, East echoing with the eight and three. West switches to the queen of hearts, and East follows with the seven when you play dummy's ace. Take it from there.

SOLUTION

It looks as though West is trying to jam your communications, having realized that the king of spades will be your ninth trick if you can reach it.

The one thing you must avoid doing at this stage is running the heart suit, for that would prepare the way for a black suit squeeze against yourself. Suppose that you discarded two diamonds and two spades on the hearts and then led a diamond. West would win and cash his other top diamond (on the bidding he is pretty sure to have them both), and you would have to make an impossible choice between throwing the king of spades and unguarding the clubs.

Since you have an entry in the nine of hearts, it must be safe at this point to lead a diamond to your jack. You can win the heart return in hand with the nine, temporarily cutting yourself off from dummy. A further diamond lead will re-establish contact and assure you of nine tricks.

FULL HAND

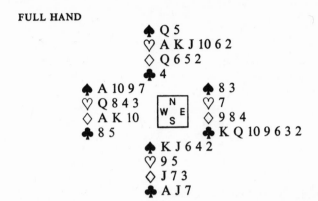

♠ Q 5
♡ A K J 10 6 2
◊ Q 6 5 2
♣ 4

♠ A 10 9 7
♡ Q 8 4 3
◊ A K 10
♣ 8 5

♠ 8 3
♡ 7
◊ 9 8 4
♣ K Q 10 9 6 3 2

♠ K J 6 4 2
♡ 9 5
◊ J 7 3
♣ A J 7

RESULT

In the other room North did not fancy the chances in three no trumps and took out to four hearts. This contract looks insecure, but in practice there is no way of defeating it and your opponents chalked up 620.

You therefore lose 1 i.m.p. if you made your contract of three no trumps, and you lose 12 i.m.p. if you went one down.

Board 3

PROBLEM

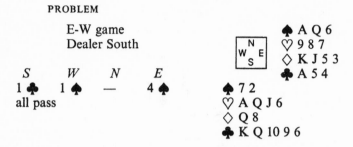

E-W game
Dealer South

S	*W*	*N*	*E*
1♣	1♠	—	4♠
all pass			

♠ A Q 6
♡ 9 8 7
◇ K J 5 3
♣ A 5 4

♠ 7 2
♡ A Q J 6
◇ Q 8
♣ K Q 10 9 6

North leads the two of clubs to the ace, ten and three. Declarer ruffs a club, leads a spade to the queen, ruffs another club and leads a spade to the ace, partner following in trumps without echoing. When the nine of hearts is led you play the ace and continue with the queen. West wins with the king and returns the ten of hearts to your jack, partner following suit. What do you lead now?

SOLUTION

Declarer's hand is easily counted as six spades, three hearts, one club, and therefore three diamonds, and it is clear that you cannot hope to defeat the contract unless partner has the ace of diamonds. Even then, you have a difficult return to make. It will not do to lead the eight of diamonds to partner's ace, for declarer will not believe that North refused to raise clubs with trump support plus the ace *and* queen of diamonds. He will play the king of diamonds on the second round and drop your queen.

You must leave declarer to tackle diamonds himself. The correct defence is to continue with the thirteenth heart. Since West cannot afford to lead a diamond from the table, he will have to ruff in hand, and North will discard a diamond. When North plays low on the diamond lead, West may well go wrong by finessing the jack to your queen. If he does the right thing by putting up dummy's king, you must unblock with the queen, hoping for partner to have the ten as well as the ace. Declarer may return to hand by means of his last trump, but partner will discard the ten of diamonds and claim the last two tricks with the diamond ace and his club.

FULL HAND

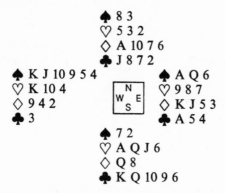

```
                    ♠ 8 3
                    ♡ 5 3 2
                    ◇ A 10 7 6
                    ♣ J 8 7 2
    ♠ K J 10 9 5 4          ♠ A Q 6
    ♡ K 10 4         N       ♡ 9 8 7
    ◇ 9 4 2       W     E    ◇ K J 5 3
    ♣ 3              S       ♣ A 5 4
                    ♠ 7 2
                    ♡ A Q J 6
                    ◇ Q 8
                    ♣ K Q 10 9 6
```

RESULT

In the other room your team-mates also played in four spades, and the play followed an identical course up to the critical point. Then South decided that a club return would be just as good as the thirteenth heart. It wasn't, and West read the position well to make his game for a score of 620.

Take 12 i.m.p. if you found the return of the thirteenth heart. Anything else gives you a flat board.

Board 4

PROBLEM

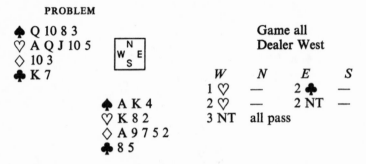

♠ Q 10 8 3
♡ A Q J 10 5
◇ 10 3
♣ K 7

Game all
Dealer West

♠ A K 4
♡ K 8 2
◇ A 9 7 5 2
♣ 8 5

W	N	E	S
1 ♡	—	2 ♣	—
2 ♡	—	2 NT	—
3 NT	all pass		

You lead the five of diamonds on which partner plays the king and declarer the six. North returns the eight of diamonds and you capture the jack with your ace. How should you continue?

SOLUTION

The obvious thing to do is to clear the diamonds, but if you give the position a little thought you will realize that this can hardly be the right defence. Declarer is marked with all the outstanding honour cards, and he is likely to have a five-card club suit. If he has two hearts he must always make his contract (with a couple of overtricks if you fail to cash your spades).

Even if East has only one heart, on a diamond continuation you will be in trouble when the clubs are run. You may throw your losing spade and the two established diamonds, but this will make the position plain to declarer. After finessing in hearts he will exit with a spade, and you will have to concede the contract by leading into the heart tenace.

Your only real chance of defeating this contract is to play East for a singleton heart and cut the link with dummy by leading a low heart at trick three. If East subsequently attacks spades you will have plenty of time to establish your diamonds, while if he runs the clubs you can discard your hearts. This defence cannot cost, for East would hardly have bid no trumps if he had a void in hearts.

FULL HAND

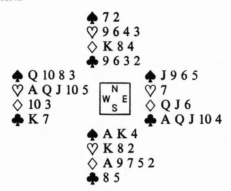

```
                    ♠ 7 2
                    ♡ 9 6 4 3
                    ◇ K 8 4
                    ♣ 9 6 3 2
    ♠ Q 10 8 3              ♠ J 9 6 5
    ♡ A Q J 10 5           ♡ 7
    ◇ 10 3                 ◇ Q J 6
    ♣ K 7                  ♣ A Q J 10 4
                    ♠ A K 4
                    ♡ K 8 2
                    ◇ A 9 7 5 2
                    ♣ 8 5
```

RESULT

In the other room your team-mates played quietly in three spades, making nine tricks for a score of 140.

The heart switch is therefore worth 6 i.m.p. to your team, while anything else results in a loss of 10 i.m.p.

Board 5

PROBLEM

♠ K 8 7 3
♡ K 8 5
◇ A K Q 2
♣ 10 4

N-S game
Dealer North

```
    N
 W     E
    S
```

♠ 6 5 2
♡ A Q 7
◇ J 9 4
♣ A J 5 2

W	N	E	S
	1 ♠	—	2 NT
—	3 NT	Dbl	all pass

West leads the nine of spades and you play low from the table. East wins with the ten and switches to the two of hearts. How do you plan the play?

SOLUTION

You have eight top tricks but it is not immediately clear where the ninth can come from. There are interesting possibilities in the black suits, however. It looks as though East may have four hearts as well as four spades, and therefore only five cards in the minor suits. If he has both the king and queen of clubs, a doubleton club honour or a singleton club, you should be able to make nine tricks in one way or another. The first move must be to play off four rounds of diamonds in order to clarify the count of the hand and perhaps force a discard from East.

The heart should be won in hand at trick two in order to preserve an entry in dummy. Then cash the diamonds, discarding a club from hand. If East discards a spade you will have no difficulty in establishing a ninth trick in spades. If East follows to four diamonds, or if he discards a club, you can cash the ace of clubs and the other top hearts and duck a spade to end-play him.

Finally, if East discards a heart you can lead the ten of clubs from the table, playing low from hand whether East covers or not. Win the club return with the ace, cash the top hearts, and lead a spade for the throw-in.

FULL HAND

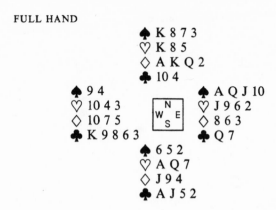

```
              ♠ K 8 7 3
              ♡ K 8 5
              ◇ A K Q 2
              ♣ 10 4
  ♠ 9 4                      ♠ A Q J 10
  ♡ 10 4 3        N         ♡ J 9 6 2
  ◇ 10 7 5     W     E      ◇ 8 6 3
  ♣ K 9 8 6 3     S         ♣ Q 7
              ♠ 6 5 2
              ♡ A Q 7
              ◇ J 9 4
              ♣ A J 5 2
```

RESULT

In the other room North opened one no trump and South raised to three no trumps. East led the two of hearts and, with no clue to the distribution, the declarer went quietly one down.

Making your doubled contract is therefore worth 13 i.m.p., while going one down costs 3 i.m.p.

Board 6

PROBLEM

E-W game
Dealer East

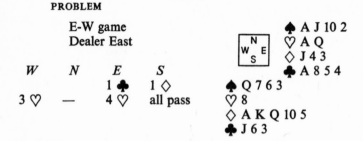

♠ A J 10 2
♡ A Q
◇ J 4 3
♣ A 8 5 4

♠ Q 7 6 3
♡ 8
◇ A K Q 10 5
♣ J 6 3

W	N	E	S
		1 ♣	1 ◇
3 ♡	—	4 ♡	all pass

Partner leads the two of diamonds, an obvious singleton. The three is played from the table and you win the trick with the ten. How should you continue?

SOLUTION

On the bidding declarer is likely to have seven good trumps, which gives him nine tricks on top. The king of either black suit would provide a tenth trick, so you must hope for partner to have the missing kings.

But there is a further danger. If given the chance, declarer may be able to create his tenth trick by ruffing his fourth diamond in dummy. In order to prevent this you should switch to your trump at trick two.

Declarer will probably win in dummy with the ace and lead another diamond, and you can then give your partner a nudge in the right direction by playing the five. If North ruffs this trick and returns his last trump, careful discarding should hold declarer to nine tricks.

FULL HAND

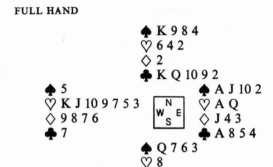

♠ K 9 8 4
♥ 6 4 2
♦ 2
♣ K Q 10 9 2

♠ 5   ♠ A J 10 2
♥ K J 10 9 7 5 3   ♥ A Q
♦ 9 8 7 6   ♦ J 4 3
♣ 7   ♣ A 8 5 4

♠ Q 7 6 3
♥ 8
♦ A K Q 10 5
♣ J 6 3

RESULT

The bidding was the same in the other room, as was the opening
lead. South thought he could afford to cash a second diamond before
switching to his trump, however, and this made a big difference to
the result. Declarer won the trump switch in dummy with the ace of
hearts and led the knave of diamonds on which South played the
five. North duly ruffed and led his last trump, and West overtook the
queen with his king. He then cashed two more trumps, discarding a
club and a spade from the table.

The fourth round of trumps applied pressure to South, who had
to reduce to two cards in one of the black suits. He chose to let go a
club, whereupon West led a club to the ace, ruffed a club, and ran
his remaining trumps for a double squeeze. North had to keep a
club, South a diamond, and neither could retain two spades.

You have therefore earned 12 i.m.p. if you switched to your
trump at trick two. Otherwise it is a flat board.

Board 7

PROBLEM

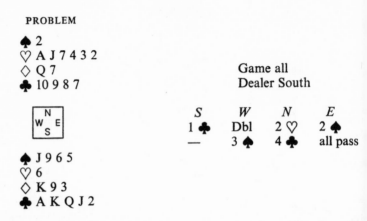

♠ 2
♡ A J 7 4 3 2
◇ Q 7
♣ 10 9 8 7

Game all
Dealer South

S	W	N	E
1 ♣	Dbl	2 ♡	2 ♠
—	3 ♠	4 ♣	all pass

♠ J 9 6 5
♡ 6
◇ K 9 3
♣ A K Q J 2

West leads the king of hearts to dummy's ace, East following with the eight. At trick two you lead a small heart and ruff high, but the prospect of establishing the suit vanishes when East discards the two of diamonds. How should you continue?

SOLUTION

Since you cannot establish the hearts you will have to rely on a cross-ruff. To make the contract you need to score either three ruffs in dummy or four in your own hand, and you must also make sure of your diamond trick. The timing of your plays needs a little thought, however. You are lucky to have avoided an initial trump lead, but you may be sure that the defenders will return a trump every time you let them in. That means that you cannot afford to give up an early trick in both diamonds and spades. If you could slip past the ace of diamonds you would be all right, for you could then concede a spade trick.

West is likely to have the ace of diamonds, but there is no need to bank on it. The safe play at trick three is the king of diamonds from hand. If either defender wins and returns a trump, you can win in dummy, ruff a heart, cross to the queen of diamonds, ruff another heart, return to dummy with a diamond ruff and ruff a further heart with your last trump.

If the king of diamonds is allowed to win at trick three, of course, you can simply concede a spade and then cross-ruff for ten tricks.

FULL HAND

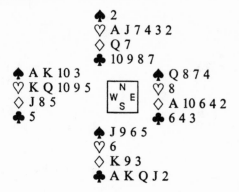

```
                    ♠ 2
                    ♡ A J 7 4 3 2
                    ◇ Q 7
                    ♣ 10 9 8 7
♠ A K 10 3                        ♠ Q 8 7 4
♡ K Q 10 9 5         N           ♡ 8
◇ J 8 5           W     E        ◇ A 10 6 4 2
♣ 5                  S           ♣ 6 4 3
                    ♠ J 9 6 5
                    ♡ 6
                    ◇ K 9 3
                    ♣ A K Q J 2
```

RESULT

In the other room your team-mates were allowed to play in three spades. On repeated club leads this went one down for a loss of 100 points.

You therefore gain 1 i.m.p. if you made four clubs, and you lose 5 i.m.p. if you went one down.

B

Board 8

PROBLEM

Love all
Dealer West

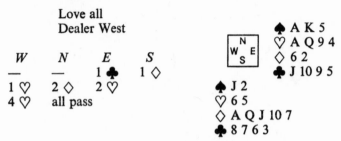

				♠ A K 5
				♡ A Q 9 4
				◇ 6 2
W	*N*	*E*	*S*	♣ J 10 9 5
—	—	1 ♣	1 ◇	
1 ♡	2 ◇	2 ♡		
4 ♡	all pass			

♠ J 2
♡ 6 5
◇ A Q J 10 7
♣ 8 7 6 3

North leads the nine of diamonds to your ace, West following
with the three. How should you continue?

SOLUTION

The opening lead marks the king of diamonds in the West hand, and
it is clear that there is not likely to be a trump trick for the defence.
That means that partner will need to score a spade trick as well as a
couple of clubs if the contract is to be defeated. This is not the occasion for a passive trump return or diamond continuation. The spades
must be attacked at once, before discards become available on
dummy's clubs.

The orthodox lead from a doubleton holding is, of course, the top
card, but that may not be good enough here. You will never be on
lead again, and if you waste the power of your jack of spades
partner may be unable to continue the spade attack when he subsequently gains the lead in clubs. You have to cater for the possibility
of partner having the queen and nine of spades, not just the queen
and ten, and the way to do that is by switching to the two of spades
at trick two.

FULL HAND

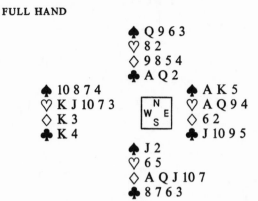

                        ♠ Q 9 6 3
                        ♡ 8 2
                        ◇ 9 8 5 4
                        ♣ A Q 2

        ♠ 10 8 7 4   ♠ A K 5
        ♡ K J 10 7 3   ♡ A Q 9 4
        ◇ K 3   ◇ 6 2
        ♣ K 4   ♣ J 10 9 5

                        ♠ J 2
                        ♡ 6 5
                        ◇ A Q J 10 7
                        ♣ 8 7 6 3

By preserving the jack of spades you make it safe for partner to return a small spade when he wins the first round of clubs, thus establishing a fourth trick for the defence.

RESULT

In the other room your team-mates also played in four hearts, and North found the deadly opening lead of the three of spades. This gave declarer no chance and the contract went one down.

You needed to find the return of the two of spades to tie the board, therefore. Anything else results in a loss of 10 i.m.p.

SCORECARD

	Maximum Gain + −	Maximum Loss + −	Your Score + −
Board 1	11	11	
2	1	12	
3	12		
4	6	10	
5	13	3	
6	12		
7	1	5	
8		10	
Total C/F	55 1	51	
Net Score	54	51	

You are allowed only a few moments to compare scores and discuss the results. The first eight boards have gone rather slowly, as usual, and the officials are anxious not to fall too far behind schedule. The captain gives you a nod and you return to your seats for the next set of boards.

SECOND SESSION

Boards 9 to 16

PROBLEMS

Board 9

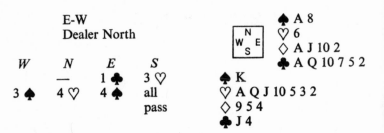

			♠ A 8
E-W			♡ 6
Dealer North			◇ A J 10 2
			♣ A Q 10 7 5 2

W	N	E	S
—		1 ♣	3 ♡
3 ♠	4 ♡	4 ♠	all
			pass

♠ K
♡ A Q J 10 5 3 2
◇ 9 5 4
♣ J 4

North leads the four of hearts to your ace, West playing the seven. How should you continue?

Solution on page 42

Board 10

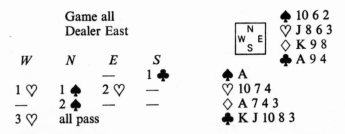

			♠ 10 6 2
Game all			♡ J 8 6 3
Dealer East			◇ K 9 8
			♣ A 9 4

W	N	E	S
—		—	1 ♣
1 ♡	1 ♠	2 ♡	—
—	2 ♠	—	—
3 ♡	all pass		

♠ A
♡ 10 7 4
◇ A 7 4 3
♣ K J 10 8 3

North leads the queen of clubs to dummy's ace. Declarer draws trumps with the ace, king and queen, North showing out on the second round and discarding the five and four of spades. A club is led to the nine and your ten, and when you continue with the king of clubs North discards the eight of spades. The ace of spades draws the three from declarer and the nine from partner. What now?

Solution on page 44

Board 11

♠ J 6 5
♡ 10 6 3
◇ Q 8 5
♣ K 8 4 2

Love all
Dealer South

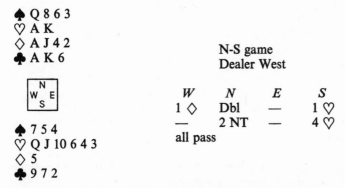

♠ A Q 4
♡ A Q J 9 7 4
◇ A K
♣ A 5

S	W	N	E
2 ♣	—	2 ◇	—
2 ♡	—	3 ♡	—
3 ♠	—	3 NT	—
4 ♣	—	5 ♣	—
6 ♡	all pass		

West leads the jack of clubs against your slam. How do you plan the play?

Solution on page 46

Board 12

♠ Q 8 6 3
♡ A K
◇ A J 4 2
♣ A K 6

N-S game
Dealer West

♠ 7 5 4
♡ Q J 10 6 4 3
◇ 5
♣ 9 7 2

W	N	E	S
1 ◇	Dbl	—	1 ♡
—	2 NT	—	4 ♡
all pass			

West leads the ten of clubs to dummy's ace, East following with the eight. You cash the ace and king of hearts and East discards the five of clubs on the second round. How should you continue?

Solution on page 48

Board 13

♠ K 4
♡ Q 8 7 3
◇ A 8 6 4
♣ Q 5 2

Game all
Dealer North

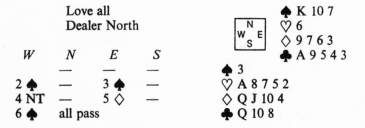

W	N	E	S
—	—		1 ♠
2 ♡	Dbl	3 ◇	3 ♠
—	4 ♠	all pass	

♠ Q 10 9 7 6 3 2
♡ K 5
◇ 3
♣ A K 7

West starts with the ace and another heart, and East ruffs the second round with the five of spades. East returns the king of diamonds to dummy's ace. How should you proceed?

Solution on page 50

Board 14

Love all
Dealer North

♠ K 10 7
♡ 6
◇ 9 7 6 3
♣ A 9 5 4 3

W	N	E	S
—	—	—	
2 ♠	—	3 ♠	—
4 NT	—	5 ◇	—
6 ♠	all pass		

♠ 3
♡ A 8 7 5 2
◇ Q J 10 4
♣ Q 10 8

North leads the queen of hearts and West plays the nine under your ace. How should you continue?

Solution on page 52

Board 15

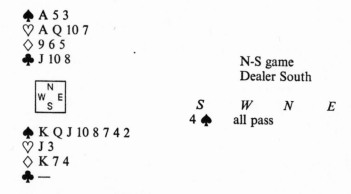

♠ A 5 3
♡ A Q 10 7
◇ 9 6 5
♣ J 10 8

N-S game
Dealer South

♠ K Q J 10 8 7 4 2
♡ J 3
◇ K 7 4
♣ —

S	W	N	E
4 ♠	all pass		

West leads the ace of clubs and partner puts down a pleasing dummy. How do you plan the play?

Solution on page 54

Board 16

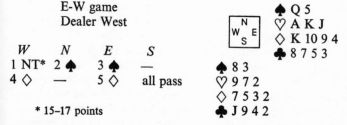

E-W game
Dealer West

♠ Q 5
♡ A K J
◇ K 10 9 4
♣ 8 7 5 3

♠ 8 3
♡ 9 7 2
◇ 7 5 3 2
♣ J 9 4 2

W	N	E	S
1 NT*	2 ♠	3 ♠	—
4 ◇	—	5 ◇	all pass

* 15–17 points

North cashes the ace and king of spades and continues with the jack of spades which is ruffed with the ten of diamonds. What do you discard?

Solution on page 56

SOLUTIONS AND RESULTS

Board 9

PROBLEM

E-W game
Dealer North

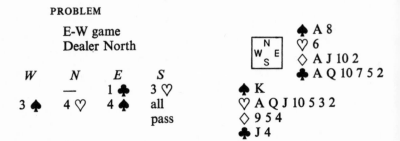

				♠ A 8
				♡ 6
				◇ A J 10 2
				♣ A Q 10 7 5 2
W	*N*	*E*	*S*	
—	1 ♣	3 ♡		♠ K
3 ♠	4 ♡	4 ♠	all	♡ A Q J 10 5 3 2
			pass	◇ 9 5 4
				♣ J 4

North leads the four of hearts to your ace, West playing the seven. How should you continue?

SOLUTION

It is far from easy to see where you can find three more tricks in defence. There can certainly be nothing for you in clubs, and it is hardly possible for partner to produce the king and queen of diamonds as well as two trump tricks. That would leave West with no more than six spades headed by the queen and ten plus the king of clubs—not really enough for a vulnerable venture at the three-level.

Minor suit honours in partner's hand are no use to the defence, so assume that declarer has these cards and credit partner with better trumps. Even though declarer is likely to have a six-card trump suit, a forcing defence may cause him to lose control and may promote three defensive trump tricks.

You should therefore continue hearts at trick two.

FULL HAND

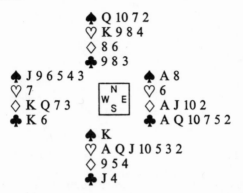

```
                    ♠ Q 10 7 2
                    ♡ K 9 8 4
                    ◇ 8 6
                    ♣ 9 8 3
    ♠ J 9 6 5 4 3              ♠ A 8
    ♡ 7              N         ♡ 6
    ◇ K Q 7 3     W   E       ◇ A J 10 2
    ♣ K 6            S         ♣ A Q 10 7 5 2
                    ♠ K
                    ♡ A Q J 10 5 3 2
                    ◇ 9 5 4
                    ♣ J 4
```

The heart continuation proves to be a killer. If declarer ruffs in dummy with the eight of spades, North scores three trump tricks by weight of cards. West fares no better if he ruffs in hand and plays on trumps. North captures the eight of spades with his ten on the second round, and a further heart lead reduces West to two trumps. Again North cannot be prevented from scoring three trump tricks.

RESULT

In the other room it was made equally difficult for your team-mates to reach their minor suit game. East elected to take a sure profit by doubling four hearts, however. This brought in 300 points for your side.

Defeating four spades is therefore worth 9 i.m.p., while allowing the game to make loses 8 i.m.p.

Board 10

PROBLEM

Game all
Dealer East

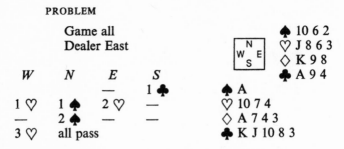

♠ 10 6 2
♡ J 8 6 3
◇ K 9 8
♣ A 9 4

W	N	E	S
		—	1 ♣
1 ♡	1 ♠	2 ♡	—
—	2 ♠	—	—
3 ♡	all pass		

♠ A
♡ 10 7 4
◇ A 7 4 3
♣ K J 10 8 3

North leads the queen of clubs to dummy's ace. Declarer draws trumps with the ace, king and queen, North showing out on the second round and discarding the five and four of spades. A club is led to the nine and your ten, and when you continue with the king of clubs North discards the eight of spades. The ace of spades draws the three from declarer and the nine from partner. What now?

SOLUTION

From the discards it is clear that your partner started with six spades, which marks declarer with three spades and two diamonds. It seems certain that at least one of West's remaining spades is a loser, but this fifth trick for the defence may not be easy to reach. It is not safe to play the ace and another diamond, for instance, for this will give declarer two tricks in the suit if he has the queen. Equally, it is unsafe to lead another club, for the ruff and discard may well give the declarer his ninth trick.

We are left with the lead of a low diamond, which is the correct defence at this point. It will defeat the contract whenever it can be defeated.

FULL HAND

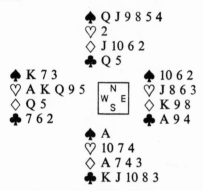

```
                    ♠ Q J 9 8 5 4
                    ♡ 2
                    ◇ J 10 6 2
                    ♣ Q 5
    ♠ K 7 3                        ♠ 10 6 2
    ♡ A K Q 9 5      N             ♡ J 8 6 3
    ◇ Q 5         W     E          ◇ K 9 8
    ♣ 7 6 2          S             ♣ A 9 4
                    ♠ A
                    ♡ 10 7 4
                    ◇ A 7 4 3
                    ♣ K J 10 8 3
```

On the return of a low diamond declarer is unable to make more than eight tricks, whether he wins in his own hand or on the table.

RESULT

Also in three hearts on the same lead, your team-mate in the West seat managed the play rather better. Winning with the ace of clubs, he cashed the ace and king of hearts, led the nine of hearts to the jack, and returned a diamond to his queen. He then exited in clubs, and South was compelled to yield the ninth trick in one way or another.

Take 6 i.m.p. if you found the return of a low diamond. Otherwise it is a flat board.

Board 11

PROBLEM

♠ J 6 5
♡ 10 6 3
♢ Q 8 5
♣ K 8 4 2

Love all
Dealer South

```
        N
    W       E
        S
```

♠ A Q 4
♡ A Q J 9 7 4
♢ A K
♣ A 5

S	W	N	E
2 ♣	—	2 ♢	—
2 ♡	—	3 ♡	—
3 ♠	—	3 NT	—
4 ♣	—	5 ♣	—
6 ♡	all pass		

West leads the jack of clubs against your slam. How do you plan the play?

SOLUTION

This problem is an exercise in percentage play. The obvious line is to win the first trick in dummy with the king of clubs and run the ten of hearts, unblocking the seven from hand if East plays low. Barring a 4–0 trump break, this play will succeed whenever East has the king of hearts. When West has the king of hearts, you will still have a chance if the trumps are 2–2. After drawing the second round of trumps, you will cash the ace and king of diamonds, enter dummy by leading the four of hearts to the six, discard your small spade on the queen of diamonds, and try the spade finesse for your contract. The total chance of success for this line of play is in the region of 55 per cent.

But a better line of play is to lead a spade for a finesse of the queen at trick two. If the finesse wins, you can cash the top diamonds and lead the queen of trumps from hand. Provided that the trumps break no worse than 3–1, you will eventually gain access to dummy with the ten of hearts and discard your losing spade on the queen of diamonds. If the spade finesse loses, the jack of spades will always serve as an entry for you to try the trump finesse. The total chance of success for this line of play is nearly 70 per cent.

FULL HAND

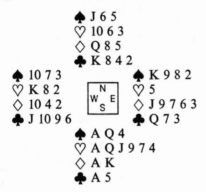

```
              ♠ J 6 5
              ♡ 10 6 3
              ◇ Q 8 5
              ♣ K 8 4 2
♠ 10 7 3                    ♠ K 9 8 2
♡ K 8 2          N          ♡ 5
◇ 10 4 2      W   E         ◇ J 9 7 6 3
♣ J 10 9 6        S         ♣ Q 7 3
              ♠ A Q 4
              ♡ A Q J 9 7 4
              ◇ A K
              ♣ A 5
```

RESULT

The contract and the opening lead were the same in the other room, and declarer adopted the inferior line of playing on trumps first. Justice was served when he went one down.

You therefore gain 14 i.m.p. if you made the slam.

Board 12

PROBLEM

♠ Q 8 6 3
♡ A K
◇ A J 4 2
♣ A K 6

N-S game
Dealer West

```
N
W   E
S
```

♠ 7 5 4
♡ Q J 10 6 4 3
◇ 5
♣ 9 7 2

W	N	E	S
1 ◇	Dbl	—	1 ♡
—	2 NT	—	4 ♡
all pass			

West leads the ten of clubs to dummy's ace, East following with the eight. You cash the ace and king of hearts and East discards the five of clubs on the second round. How should you continue?

SOLUTION

With nine top tricks you will need to seek the tenth in spades. West is likely to have the top spades as well as the king and queen of diamonds for his opening bid, but the 4–1 trump break creates a problem. If you cash the ace of diamonds, ruff a diamond, draw trumps and lead a spade, West will be able to force out your last trump before you can establish your spade trick.

It would be helpful if you could concede a trick to the defence at this point, but you must avoid giving the lead to East, for all the indications are that West is very short in clubs. The way to retain control is to lead the jack of diamonds from the table at trick four. This places the lead firmly in the West hand, avoiding the risk of a ruff. You can ruff the diamond return, draw trumps, discarding a club and a spade from dummy, and lead a spade. Ruff the next diamond and lead another spade to make dummy high.

FULL HAND

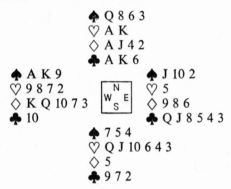

```
                    ♠ Q 8 6 3
                    ♡ A K
                    ◇ A J 4 2
                    ♣ A K 6
    ♠ A K 9                        ♠ J 10 2
    ♡ 9 8 7 2          N           ♡ 5
    ◇ K Q 10 7 3     W   E         ◇ 9 8 6
    ♣ 10               S           ♣ Q J 8 5 4 3
                    ♠ 7 5 4
                    ♡ Q J 10 6 4 3
                    ◇ 5
                    ♣ 9 7 2
```

RESULT

In the other room West led the king of diamonds against the same
contract, giving the declarer a somewhat easier task. South won with
the ace, cashed the ace and king of hearts, ruffed a diamond, drew
trumps and led a spade. West won and exited with his club. The
declarer won with the ace, ruffed a diamond with his last trump and
led another spade. On winning the trick, however, West was able to
cash two diamonds to put the contract one down.

Declarer missed a number of chances, of course. He could have
succeeded by the double-dummy play of ducking the first diamond
or, more reasonably, by cashing a top club before ruffing a diamond
in hand. Even after leaving West with an exit card in clubs, South
could have made his contract by cashing the second top club. In
order to keep his spade honour guarded West would have had to
shed a diamond, whereupon a diamond ruff and a further spade lead
would have ensured a tenth trick for declarer.

Take 12 i.m.p. if you found the difficult play of the jack of diamonds at trick four.

Board 13

PROBLEM

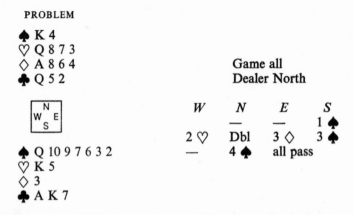

♠ K 4
♡ Q 8 7 3
◇ A 8 6 4
♣ Q 5 2

Game all
Dealer North

	W	N	E	S
	—	—		1 ♠
	2 ♡	Dbl	3 ◇	3 ♠
	—	4 ♠	all pass	

♠ Q 10 9 7 6 3 2
♡ K 5
◇ 3
♣ A K 7

West starts with the ace and another heart, and East ruffs the second round with the five of spades. East returns the king of diamonds to dummy's ace. How should you proceed?

SOLUTION

In spite of suffering a ruff, you are still a heavy favourite to make your contract. The only problem is to avoid losing two more trump tricks. The bidding marks the ace of spades in the West hand, and a lead of the king of spades at this point will be fatal if West has all the remaining trumps.

How can you find out if this is the position? Quite simply, by leading the queen of hearts from the table at trick four. East is bound to ruff if he can find another trump in his hand, because for all he knows you may be hoping to discard a losing diamond on the queen of hearts. It follows that if East fails to ruff you should ruff the queen of hearts yourself and run the ten of spades through West.

FULL HAND

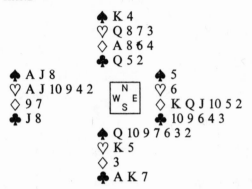

```
               ♠ K 4
               ♡ Q 8 7 3
               ◇ A 8 6 4
               ♣ Q 5 2
♠ A J 8                      ♠ 5
♡ A J 10 9 4 2    N          ♡ 6
◇ 9 7          W     E       ◇ K Q J 10 5 2
♣ J 8             S          ♣ 10 9 6 4 3
               ♠ Q 10 9 7 6 3 2
               ♡ K 5
               ◇ 3
               ♣ A K 7
```

RESULT

The contract was the same in the other room, but West was unable to find the inspired lead of the ace of hearts. He led the nine of diamonds and the declarer made ten tricks without breathing hard.

You therefore needed to finesse against the jack of spades to achieve a flat board. Minus 12 i.m.p. if you failed.

Board 14

PROBLEM

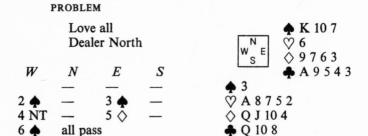

				♠ K 10 7
	Love all			♡ 6
	Dealer North			◇ 9 7 6 3
				♣ A 9 5 4 3
W	*N*	*E*	*S*	
—	—	—		♠ 3
2 ♠	—	3 ♠	—	♡ A 8 7 5 2
4 NT	—	5 ◇	—	◇ Q J 10 4
6 ♠	all pass			♣ Q 10 8

North leads the queen of hearts and West plays the nine under your ace. How should you continue?

SOLUTION

Clearly the diamond suit is the one most likely to provide the setting trick, but there can be no good reason for switching to a diamond at trick two. West has bid the slam with confidence and with the aid of Blackwood. He will certainly not be missing a second ace.

On this hand the diamonds can wait. You must get your priorities right by turning your attention to the threat of the long club suit in dummy. If declarer has a singleton club he may be able to establish a second trick in the suit, and that may be all he needs for his slam.

The way to avert this danger is by returning your trump at trick two. This will remove one of dummy's entries prematurely, and declarer will be unable to get the clubs going unless he has the king.

FULL HAND

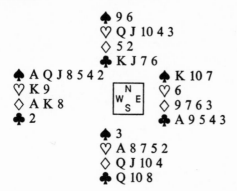

```
              ♠ 9 6
              ♡ Q J 10 4 3
              ◇ 5 2
              ♣ K J 7 6
♠ A Q J 8 5 4 2              ♠ K 10 7
♡ K 9          N            ♡ 6
◇ A K 8      W   E          ◇ 9 7 6 3
♣ 2            S            ♣ A 9 5 4 3
              ♠ 3
              ♡ A 8 7 5 2
              ◇ Q J 10 4
              ♣ Q 10 8
```

RESULT

Your team-mates in the other room managed to avoid this dubious slam, playing in four spades and making a couple of overtricks for a score of 480.

A swing of 22 i.m.p. thus depended on your card at trick two. Plus 11 for leading your trump, and minus 11 for leading anything else.

Board 15

PROBLEM

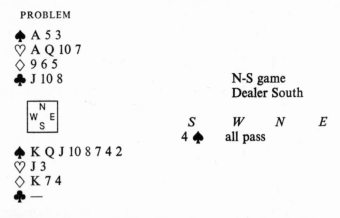

♠ A 5 3
♡ A Q 10 7
◇ 9 6 5
♣ J 10 8

N-S game
Dealer South

S	W	N	E
4 ♠	all pass		

♠ K Q J 10 8 7 4 2
♡ J 3
◇ K 7 4
♣ —

West leads the ace of clubs. How do you plan the play?

SOLUTION

You have nine top tricks and excellent chances of making more, but there is some danger of losing a heart and three tricks in diamonds. What you have to look for is a means of avoiding that hazardous heart finesse. Is it possible to develop a second heart trick without allowing East to gain the lead?

Once you ask yourself the question, the answer is fairly obvious. Just allow West to win the first trick with the ace of clubs, discarding a heart from hand. You can win a heart switch with the ace and draw two rounds of trumps, finishing in dummy and taking care to preserve the two of spades in your hand. Then run the queen of hearts, discarding a diamond unless East produces the king. Ten tricks are thus guaranteed.

FULL HAND

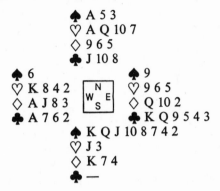

```
                    ♠ A 5 3
                    ♡ A Q 10 7
                    ◇ 9 6 5
                    ♣ J 10 8
     ♠ 6                        ♠ 9
     ♡ K 8 4 2    ┌─────┐       ♡ 9 6 5
     ◇ A J 8 3    │  N  │       ◇ Q 10 2
     ♣ A 7 6 2    │W   E│       ♣ K Q 9 5 4 3
                  │  S  │
                  └─────┘
                    ♠ K Q J 10 8 7 4 2
                    ♡ J 3
                    ◇ K 7 4
                    ♣ —
```

RESULT

There is no justice. Playing in the same contract in the other room, your opponent in the South seat took the risk of going down and finished with two overtricks. He ruffed the opening club lead, drew trumps with the king, and ran the jack of hearts successfully. Six more rounds of trumps compelled West to bare his ace of diamonds in order to keep three hearts. After repeating the heart finesse, South threw West in with a diamond and made the last two tricks on the forced heart return.

Correct play therefore loses 2 i.m.p. on this board, while inaccurate play gives you a tie.

Board 16

PROBLEM

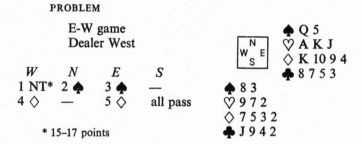

E-W game
Dealer West

W	N	E	S
1 NT*	2 ♠	3 ♠	—
4 ◇	—	5 ◇	all pass

* 15–17 points

♠ Q 5
♡ A K J
◇ K 10 9 4
♣ 8 7 5 3

♠ 8 3
♡ 9 7 2
◇ 7 5 3 2
♣ J 9 4 2

North cashes the ace and king of spades and continues with the jack of spades which is ruffed with the ten of diamonds. What do you discard?

SOLUTION

From the bidding it is probable that the declarer has a 3-3-4-3 distribution. If West has his quota of 15 points, partner can have no more than 3 points outside the spade suit. If he has the king or queen of clubs the contract is likely to go down, while if he has the singleton queen of diamonds the contract will surely be made.

The critical case is where partner has the queen of hearts. The declarer will then have eleven easy tricks with the aid of the heart finesse—unless you can persuade him that the heart finesse will fail. The way to do that is to under-ruff at trick three, hoping to give the impression that you can be squeezed in hearts and clubs. If the declarer has the ten of hearts he may see an alternative to the heart finesse in a criss-cross squeeze.

FULL HAND

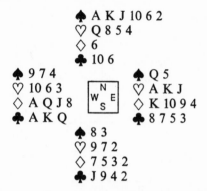

              ♠ A K J 10 6 2
              ♡ Q 8 5 4
              ◇ 6
              ♣ 10 6
    ♠ 9 7 4   ♠ Q 5
    ♡ 10 6 3   ┌─────┐   ♡ A K J
    ◇ A Q J 8   │ W N E │   ◇ K 10 9 4
    ♣ A K Q   │   S   │   ♣ 8 7 5 3
                  └─────┘
              ♠ 8 3
              ♡ 9 7 2
              ◇ 7 5 3 2
              ♣ J 9 4 2

When you under-ruff, declarer is likely to play you for four clubs
and the guarded queen of hearts. After drawing trumps he will cash
one high heart, two high clubs, and then lead his last trump, discarding the jack of hearts from the table. When you discard a heart he will
lead a heart to the table, confidently expecting your queen to fall. It
will take the whole of the lunch-break for him to recover from the
shock when it does not.

RESULT

You are booked for a poor result anyway, for in the other room
West raised directly to three no trumps over the intervening bid of
two spades. North gratefully cashed the first six tricks to put the
contract two down.

Chalk up minus 3 i.m.p. if you discarded a trump at trick three.
and minus 13 if you did not.

SCORECARD

B/F	Maximum Gain +	Maximum Gain −	Maximum Loss +	Maximum Loss −	Your Score +	Your Score −
	55	1		51		
Board 9	9			8		
10	6					
11	14					
12	12					
13				12		
14	11			11		
15				2		
16		3		13		
Total C/F	107	4		97		
Net Score	103			97		

The time is 1.20 as you finish scoring and you have to restart at 2.15. Even allowing for slow service in the dining-room there is time for an omelet or something of the sort. Your captain orders water all round and waves the wine waiter away.

During the meal the talk is about the crazy bids and plays made by the opponents, and the brilliancies that might have been. Nothing is said about the crazy efforts by your own side. That will come later, after the match.

As the time draws near, the captain informs you that your services are required for the next eight boards. You step out for a quick breath of fresh air before returning to the playing-rooms for the next session.

THIRD SESSION

Boards 17 to 24

PROBLEMS

Board 17

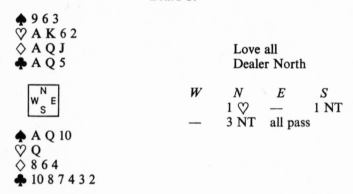

♠ 9 6 3
♡ A K 6 2
◇ A Q J
♣ A Q 5

♠ A Q 10
♡ Q
◇ 8 6 4
♣ 10 8 7 4 3 2

Love all
Dealer North

W	N	E	S
	1 ♡	—	1 NT
—	3 NT	all pass	

West leads the eight of spades and you capture the king with your ace. How should you proceed?

Solution on page 64

Board 18

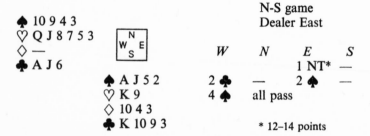

♠ 10 9 4 3
♡ Q J 8 7 5 3
◇ —
♣ A J 6

♠ A J 5 2
♡ K 9
◇ 10 4 3
♣ K 10 9 3

N-S game
Dealer East

W	N	E	S
		1 NT*	—
2 ♣	—	2 ♠	—
4 ♠	all pass		

* 12–14 points

Your lead of the three of diamonds is ruffed in dummy, partner playing the nine and declarer the two. The ten of spades is covered by the queen and king, and you let declarer win the trick. East ruffs the six of diamonds in dummy, partner completing an echo with the eight. Then comes the queen of hearts, on which North plays the two, East the four and you the king. How should you continue?

Solution on page 66

Board 19

♠ Q 7 4
♡ K Q 5
◇ Q J 6 5
♣ A Q J

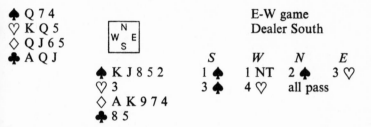

E-W game
Dealer South

S	W	N	E
1 ♠	1 NT	2 ♠	3 ♡
3 ♠	4 ♡	all pass	

♠ K J 8 5 2
♡ 3
◇ A K 9 7 4
♣ 8 5

On your lead of the ace of diamonds North plays the three and East the eight. How should you continue?

Solution on page 68

Board 20

♠ Q 10 9 6
♡ A K Q 9 4
◇ 10 6 3
♣ 4

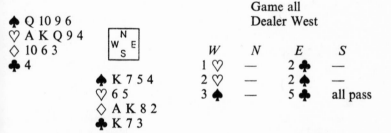

Game all
Dealer West

W	N	E	S
1 ♡	—	2 ♣	—
2 ♡	—	2 ♠	—
3 ♠	—	5 ♣	all pass

♠ K 7 5 4
♡ 6 5
◇ A K 8 2
♣ K 7 3

On your lead of the ace of diamonds North plays the queen and East the five. What now?

Solution on page 70

Board 21

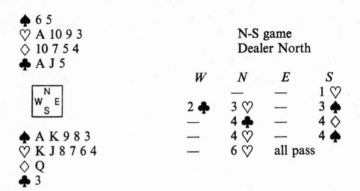

♠ 6 5
♡ A 10 9 3
♢ 10 7 5 4
♣ A J 5

N-S game
Dealer North

♠ A K 9 8 3
♡ K J 8 7 6 4
♢ Q
♣ 3

W	N	E	S
—	—	—	1 ♡
2 ♣	3 ♡	—	3 ♠
—	4 ♣	—	4 ♢
—	4 ♡	—	4 ♠
—	6 ♡	all pass	

West leads the two of diamonds against your slam. East wins with the ace and returns the three of diamonds which you ruff. Both defenders follow small when you lead a heart to dummy's ace. How should you continue?

Solution on page 72

Board 22

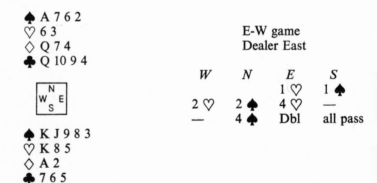

♠ A 7 6 2
♡ 6 3
♢ Q 7 4
♣ Q 10 9 4

E-W game
Dealer East

♠ K J 9 8 3
♡ K 8 5
♢ A 2
♣ 7 6 5

W	N	E	S
		1 ♡	1 ♠
2 ♡	2 ♠	4 ♡	—
—	4 ♠	Dbl	all pass

West leads the ten of hearts to his partner's ace. East cashes the ace of clubs and switches back to the queen of hearts. You win with the king, lead a spade to the ace, and return a low spade on which East plays the ten. Take it from there.

Solution on page 74

Board 23

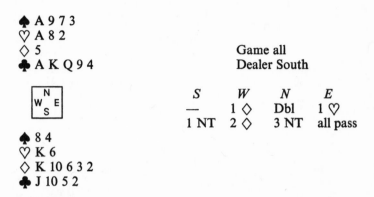

♠ A 9 7 3
♡ A 8 2
◇ 5
♣ A K Q 9 4

Game all
Dealer South

♠ 8 4
♡ K 6
◇ K 10 6 3 2
♣ J 10 5 2

S	W	N	E
—	1 ◇	Dbl	1 ♡
1 NT	2 ◇	3 NT	all pass

West leads the jack of hearts, and when you play low from dummy East overtakes with the queen. How do you plan the play?

Solution on page 76

Board 24

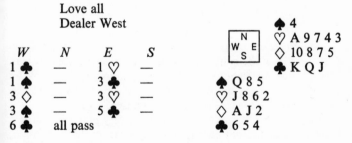

Love all
Dealer West

♠ 4
♡ A 9 7 4 3
◇ 10 8 7 5
♣ K Q J

♠ Q 8 5
♡ J 8 6 2
◇ A J 2
♣ 6 5 4

W	N	E	S
1 ♣	—	1 ♡	—
1 ♠	—	3 ♣	—
3 ◇	—	3 ♡	—
3 ♠	—	5 ♣	—
6 ♣	all pass		

North leads the three of diamonds and West plays the four under your ace. How should you continue?

Solution on page 78

SOLUTIONS AND RESULTS

Board 17

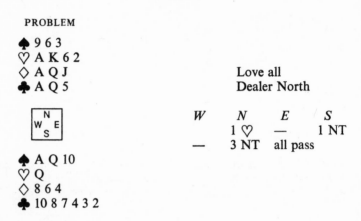

♠ 9 6 3
♡ A K 6 2
◇ A Q J
♣ A Q 5

Love all
Dealer North

W	N	E	S
	1 ♡	—	1 NT
—	3 NT	all pass	

♠ A Q 10
♡ Q
◇ 8 6 4
♣ 10 8 7 4 3 2

West leads the eight of spades and you capture the king with your ace. How should you proceed?

SOLUTION

From the opening lead it appears that the jack of spades is favourably placed, in which case the contract can be in no danger. Appearances are sometimes deceptive, however, and there is no need to bank on making three spade tricks on this hand. It would certainly be unwise to risk a finesse of the queen of clubs at trick two.

The correct move is to make the standard safety play of leading a club to the ace. If an honour card does not appear on the first round, you can return to the queen of hearts and lead another club towards dummy's queen. On this line of play the contract is not at risk unless the jack of spades and both club honours are offside.

FULL HAND

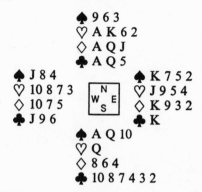

```
              ♠ 9 6 3
              ♡ A K 6 2
              ◇ A Q J
              ♣ A Q 5
  ♠ J 8 4                  ♠ K 7 5 2
  ♡ 10 8 7 3      N        ♡ J 9 5 4
  ◇ 10 7 5     W   E       ◇ K 9 3 2
  ♣ J 9 6         S        ♣ K
              ♠ A Q 10
              ♡ Q
              ◇ 8 6 4
              ♣ 10 8 7 4 3 2
```

As you see from the full diagram, West has made an unorthodox lead. If you take a losing club finesse, a spade will come back, your ten will lose to the jack, and the suit will be cleared. When West subsequently gains the lead on the third round of clubs he will switch to a diamond, and the blockage in hearts will result in your going one down.

RESULT

In the other room North opened with a bid of two no trumps and South raised to three no trumps. East led a heart, and although the declarer lost two club tricks he could not be prevented from making his contract with an overtrick.

Playing a club to the ace at trick two therefore gains 1 i.m.p. for your team, while finessing the queen of clubs loses 10 i.m.p.

C

Board 18

PROBLEM

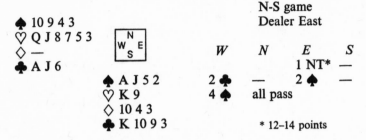

N-S game
Dealer East

♠ 10 9 4 3
♡ Q J 8 7 5 3
◇ —
♣ A J 6

♠ A J 5 2
♡ K 9
◇ 10 4 3
♣ K 10 9 3

W	N	E	S
		1 NT*	—
2♣	—	2♠	—
4♠	all pass		

* 12–14 points

Your lead of the three of diamonds is ruffed in dummy, partner
playing the nine and declarer the two. The ten of spades is covered
by the queen and king, and you let declarer win the trick. East ruffs
the six of diamonds in dummy, partner completing an echo with the
eight. Then comes the queen of hearts, on which North plays the two,
East the four and you the king. How should you continue?

SOLUTION

Clearly the contract can be defeated if partner has either the ace of
diamonds or the queen of clubs. It seems a matter of routine to cash
one top spade first in order to remove the last trump from dummy.
Then you can try diamonds and, if necessary, clubs when you next
gain the lead. This defence will not be good enough if declarer has
both key cards, however, for he will be able to draw trumps and
claim ten tricks with the aid of the established heart suit.

If you look more closely into the position, you may realize that
you can defeat the contract even if declarer has both the ace of
diamonds and the queen of clubs provided that you keep your trump
holding intact. The correct move is to return your heart with a view
to removing an entry from declarer's hand. The business of drawing
trumps will then be more than East can manage, and your fourth
trump will become the setting trick.

FULL HAND

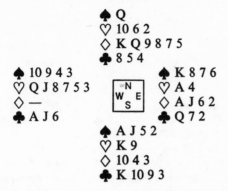

```
                        ♠ Q
                        ♡ 10 6 2
                        ◇ K Q 9 8 7 5
                        ♣ 8 5 4
        ♠ 10 9 4 3                      ♠ K 8 7 6
        ♡ Q J 8 7 5 3                   ♡ A 4
        ◇ —              N              ◇ A J 6 2
        ♣ A J 6       W     E           ♣ Q 7 2
                        S
                        ♠ A J 5 2
                        ♡ K 9
                        ◇ 10 4 3
                        ♣ K 10 9 3
```

RESULT

You are booked for a gain on the board, for in the other room your
team-mates were allowed to make four spades doubled on indifferent
defence.

Take 12 i.m.p. for returning the nine of hearts, and 5 i.m.p. for
leading anything else.

Board 19

PROBLEM

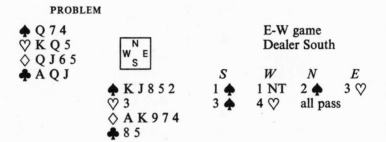

	S	W	N	E
	1 ♠	1 NT	2 ♠	3 ♡
	3 ♠	4 ♡	all pass	

♠ Q 7 4
♡ K Q 5
◇ Q J 6 5
♣ A Q J

E-W game
Dealer South

♠ K J 8 5 2
♡ 3
◇ A K 9 7 4
♣ 8 5

On your lead of the ace of diamonds North plays the three and East the eight. How should you continue?

SOLUTION

First you have to analyse the diamond position. Partner would not have played the three from 10-3-2, and must therefore have either a doubleton or a singleton. But if the three is a singleton, why should East play the eight? The sensible course for him would be to play the two in the hope that you would switch. It appears almost certain that the diamonds are 2–2, and it is clear that you must take what tricks you can in spades before declarer can get discards on the diamonds.

Partner is likely to have one high card, which may be in spades, clubs or trumps. There can be no hurry for a spade lead even if partner has the ace, for you will have another chance to lead spades when you are in with the king of diamonds. A club switch is unlikely to work even if partner has the king. Declarer will go up with the ace, draw trumps, and establish diamonds for a spade discard.

By a process of elimination you are forced to the conclusion that a trump switch is needed if you are to retain all your options. If partner has the ace of trumps he will switch to spades and perhaps set up a fourth defensive trick.

FULL HAND

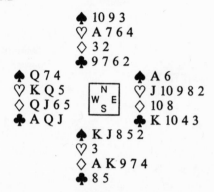

```
              ♠ 10 9 3
              ♡ A 7 6 4
              ◇ 3 2
              ♣ 9 7 6 2
  ♠ Q 7 4                  ♠ A 6
  ♡ K Q 5      ┌──────┐    ♡ J 10 9 8 2
  ◇ Q J 6 5    │ N    │    ◇ 10 8
  ♣ A Q J      │W   E │    ♣ K 10 4 3
               │  S   │
               └──────┘
              ♠ K J 8 5 2
              ♡ 3
              ◇ A K 9 7 4
              ♣ 8 5
```

RESULT

In the other room your team-mates reached the unbeatable contract of three no trumps, but the opponents sacrificed in four spades. This was doubled and went two down on a trump lead to give your team 300 points.

The trump switch at trick two is therefore worth 9 i.m.p., while anything else results in a loss of 8 i.m.p.

Board 20

PROBLEM

♠ Q 10 9 6
♡ A K Q 9 4
◇ 10 6 3
♣ 4

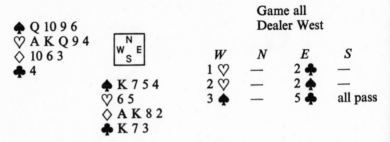

Game all
Dealer West

♠ K 7 5 4
♡ 6 5
◇ A K 8 2
♣ K 7 3

W	N	E	S
1 ♡	—	2 ♣	—
2 ♡	—	2 ♠	—
3 ♣	—	5 ♣	all pass

On your lead of the ace of diamonds North plays the queen and East the five. What now?

SOLUTION

The play of the queen of diamonds announces possession of the jack, and it is tempting to continue with a small diamond at trick two. If you could put partner on lead, a spade return would defeat the contract by at least two tricks.

That would be a reasonable defence if the contract were four clubs, but against five clubs you do not need a second diamond trick. On the assumption that declarer has no more than seven clubs, you can make certain of defeating the contract by switching to a heart at trick two.

East's failure to support hearts marks him with no more than two cards in the suit, and when you are in with the king of clubs you can complete the job of severing communications by leading your second heart. Declarer is thus prevented from enjoying more than two heart tricks, and the king of spades is bound to score the setting trick.

FULL HAND

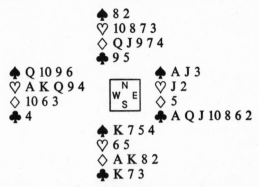

```
                    ♠ 8 2
                    ♡ 10 8 7 3
                    ◇ Q J 9 7 4
                    ♣ 9 5
    ♠ Q 10 9 6                    ♠ A J 3
    ♡ A K Q 9 4      N            ♡ J 2
    ◇ 10 6 3      W     E         ◇ 5
    ♣ 4              S            ♣ A Q J 10 8 6 2
                    ♠ K 7 5 4
                    ♡ 6 5
                    ◇ A K 8 2
                    ♣ K 7 3
```

Note that on a diamond continuation declarer can ruff, knock out the king of trumps, and eventually discard his losing spades on the hearts.

RESULT

In the other room your team-mates reached a contract of four hearts, and West made it by careful play. Ruffing the second diamond with the two of hearts, he cashed the jack of hearts and led the three of spades from the table. The defenders were thus restricted to two diamond tricks and one black king.

Take 12 i.m.p. if you switched to a heart at trick two. You still pick up 1 i.m.p. if you did not.

Board 21

PROBLEM

♠ 6 5
♡ A 10 9 3
◇ 10 7 5 4
♣ A J 5

N-S game
Dealer North

W	N	E	S
—	—	—	1 ♡
2 ♣	3 ♡	—	3 ♠
—	4 ♣	—	4 ◇
—	4 ♡	—	4 ♠
—	6 ♡	all pass	

♠ A K 9 8 3
♡ K J 8 7 6 4
◇ Q
♣ 3

West leads the two of diamonds against your slam. East wins with the ace and returns the three of diamonds which you ruff. Both defenders follow small when you lead a heart to dummy's ace. How should you continue?

SOLUTION

This is just a matter of normal technique to guard against a bad break in the side suit. West is known to be long in clubs, and he is marked with four diamonds by the play to the first two tricks. He is likely to be short in both spades and trumps, and you should therefore test the spades before drawing the outstanding queen of trumps. If both defenders follow to the ace and king of spades, you can cash the king of hearts and then establish the spades by ruffing twice in dummy.

The extra chance appears when West discards on the second round of spades. Now you have three trumps in dummy to take care of the three losing spades, and the slam is still made.

FULL HAND

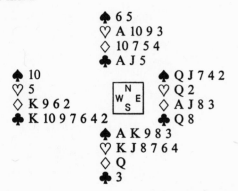

♠ 6 5
♡ A 10 9 3
◇ 10 7 5 4
♣ A J 5

♠ 10
♡ 5
◇ K 9 6 2
♣ K 10 9 7 6 4 2

♠ Q J 7 4 2
♡ Q 2
◇ A J 8 3
♣ Q 8

♠ A K 9 8 3
♡ K J 8 7 6 4
◇ Q
♣ 3

RESULT

Your opponents are not in the habit of bidding 22-point slams. In the other room they played in four hearts, making eleven tricks for a score of 650.

Making your slam is therefore worth 13 i.m.p., while going down costs 13 i.m.p.

Board 22

PROBLEM

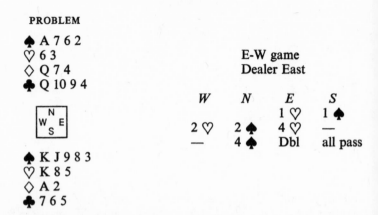

♠ A 7 6 2
♡ 6 3
◇ Q 7 4
♣ Q 10 9 4

E-W game
Dealer East

W	N	E	S
		1 ♡	1 ♠
2 ♡	2 ♠	4 ♡	—
—	4 ♠	Dbl	all pass

♠ K J 9 8 3
♡ K 8 5
◇ A 2
♣ 7 6 5

West leads the ten of hearts to his partner's ace. East cashes the ace of clubs and switches back to the queen of hearts. You win with the king, lead a spade to the ace, and return a low spade on which East plays the ten. Take it from there.

SOLUTION

No doubt you would rather be defending against four hearts, but you are in four spades doubled with a critical decision to make in the trump suit. Given that the ace of clubs is likely to be a singleton, there are two good reasons for playing for the drop in spades. In the first place, East's strong bidding is indicative of 2-5-5-1 rather than 3-5-4-1 distribution.

But the clinching argument is that the contract can never be made if the trumps are 3–1. After a successful trump finesse you may draw the last trump and lead a club, but West will not be so co-operative as to play the king. He will play low and you will be stuck in dummy with no convenient way of returning to hand. To use the ace of diamonds would create a fourth loser, and the last trump on the table is needed for ruffing a heart.

You should therefore play the king of spades and hope to drop the queen from the West hand.

FULL HAND

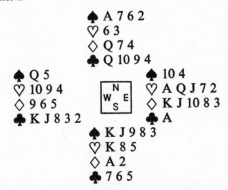

```
                    ♠ A 7 6 2
                    ♡ 6 3
                    ◇ Q 7 4
                    ♣ Q 10 9 4
  ♠ Q 5                              ♠ 10 4
  ♡ 10 9 4          ┌─────┐         ♡ A Q J 7 2
  ◇ 9 6 5          W│  N  │E        ◇ K J 10 8 3
  ♣ K J 8 3 2       │  S  │         ♣ A
                    └─────┘
                    ♠ K J 9 8 3
                    ♡ K 8 5
                    ◇ A 2
                    ♣ 7 6 5
```

An initial diamond lead would have defeated four spades easily enough. On the heart lead the defence can prevail only if East allows your king to win the first trick. After winning the ace of clubs, he can then put his partner in with the nine of hearts to lead a diamond.

RESULT

In the other room your team-mates played in four hearts, fortunately undoubled. Careful defence held the declarer to eight tricks for a loss of 200 points.

Playing for the drop in spades therefore gains 9 i.m.p. for your team, while finessing loses 11 i.m.p.

Board 23

PROBLEM

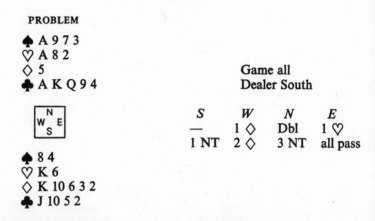

♠ A 9 7 3
♡ A 8 2
♢ 5
♣ A K Q 9 4

Game all
Dealer South

♠ 8 4
♡ K 6
♢ K 10 6 3 2
♣ J 10 5 2

S	W	N	E
—	1 ♢	Dbl	1 ♡
1 NT	2 ♢	3 NT	all pass

West leads the jack of hearts, and when you play low from dummy East overtakes with the queen. How do you plan the play?

SOLUTION

There are eight top tricks in view, and it looks as though the ninth will have to come from an end-play in diamonds. In order to prepare the ground, you must first extract West's exit cards in the other suits. At the same time, you cannot afford to let East in, for a diamond lead through your king would ruin your prospects. You have a chance of success when West has no more than two hearts and two or three spades including the king and queen.

Win the first trick with the king of hearts and lead a spade, playing a low card from dummy if West produces the king or queen. Win the next heart with the ace, return to hand with a club, and lead another spade, again ducking in dummy if the king or queen appears. Win the spade return with the ace and run the clubs, and you are ready for the end-play. Lead the singleton diamond from the table and cover East's card as cheaply as possible. If your reading of the distribution is correct, West will be able to cash two diamonds but will then have to concede a diamond trick to you.

FULL HAND

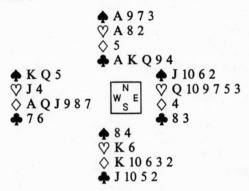

♠ A 9 7 3
♡ A 8 2
◇ 5
♣ A K Q 9 4

♠ K Q 5
♡ J 4
◇ A Q J 9 8 7
♣ 7 6

♠ J 10 6 2
♡ Q 10 9 7 5 3
◇ 4
♣ 8 3

♠ 8 4
♡ K 6
◇ K 10 6 3 2
♣ J 10 5 2

RESULT

The contract was the same in the other room, but declarer had an easy task when West led the queen of diamonds.

You therefore needed to make the contract to tie the board. Going down costs 12 i.m.p.

Board 24

PROBLEM

Love all
Dealer West

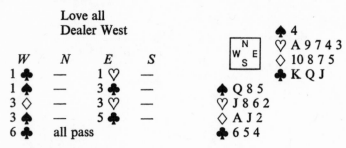

W	N	E	S
1 ♣	—	1 ♡	—
1 ♠	—	3 ♣	—
3 ◇	—	3 ♡	—
3 ♠	—	5 ♣	—
6 ♣	all pass		

♠ 4
♡ A 9 7 4 3
◇ 10 8 7 5
♣ K Q J

♠ Q 8 5
♡ J 8 6 2
◇ A J 2
♣ 6 5 4

North leads the three of diamonds and West plays the four under your ace. How should you continue?

SOLUTION

Don't insult declarer by trying for a second diamond trick. West is bound to have the king of diamonds, and also the top cards in the black suits. There appears to be no chance for the defence if declarer's distribution is 5-1-2-5. Even a trump return will not be enough to prevent him from ruffing two spades on the table.

You are reduced to hoping for a heart loser in declarer's hand, and even then there are problems ahead for the defence. If partner has the king of hearts without the queen, he will be ripe for squeezing in the red suits once the declarer has isolated the diamond menace.

You must therefore play for partner's hearts to be as good as K 10 and lead a heart at trick two to break up the squeeze.

FULL HAND

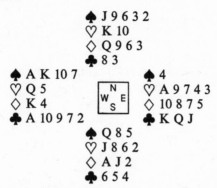

```
                    ♠ J 9 6 3 2
                    ♡ K 10
                    ◇ Q 9 6 3
                    ♣ 8 3
    ♠ A K 10 7              ♠ 4
    ♡ Q 5          N        ♡ A 9 7 4 3
    ◇ K 4        W   E      ◇ 10 8 7 5
    ♣ A 10 9 7 2   S        ♣ K Q J
                    ♠ Q 8 5
                    ♡ J 8 6 2
                    ◇ A J 2
                    ♣ 6 5 4
```

You can see what would happen on any other return. West would cash the ace of spades, ruff a spade, return to the king of diamonds, ruff another spade and ruff a diamond. The run of the trumps followed by the king of spades would then make mincemeat of North's hand, ensuring a twelfth trick for the declarer either in hearts or in diamonds.

RESULT

Your team-mates were content to play this hand in three no trumps, making nine tricks for a score of 400.

The heart switch at trick two therefore gains 10 i.m.p., while anything else loses 11 i.m.p.

SCORECARD

	Maximum Gain		Maximum Loss		Your Score	
	+	−	+	−	+	−
B/F	107	4		97		
Board 17	1			10		
18	12		5			
19	9			8		
20	12		1			
21	13			13		
22	9			11		
23				12		
24	10			11		
Total C/F	173	4	6	162		
Net Score	169			156		

When the scoring has been completed, your captain indicates that he would like you to continue and you return to your seats for the next set of boards.

FOURTH SESSION

Boards 25 to 32

PROBLEMS

Board 25

♠ Q J 5 2
♡ J 4
◇ 8 6 5 3
♣ K 10 3

E-W game
Dealer North

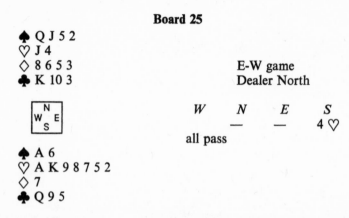

W	N	E	S
	—	—	4 ♡
all pass			

♠ A 6
♡ A K 9 8 7 5 2
◇ 7
♣ Q 9 5

On the lead of the ace of diamonds East drops the queen. West continues with the two of diamonds to his partner's ten. You ruff and cash the ace of hearts but the queen does not appear. When you continue with the king of hearts, West produces the queen and East the ten. What do you play now?

Solution on page 86

Board 26

Game all
Dealer East

♠ 8 5
♡ Q 4
◇ A K Q 8 3
♣ A 9 6 4

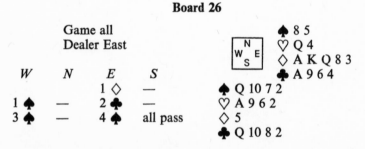

♠ Q 10 7 2
♡ A 9 6 2
◇ 5
♣ Q 10 8 2

W	N	E	S
		1 ◇	—
1 ♠	—	2 ♣	—
3 ♠	—	4 ♠	all pass

North leads the five of hearts to your ace and wins the heart return with the king, West playing the seven and the ten. Winning the diamond switch with the ace, West leads a spade to his ace, regards North's nine with suspicion, and leads another diamond to the king. After ruffing, what do you return?

Solution on page 88

Board 27

♠ K Q 6
♡ 6
◇ Q J 8 3
♣ K Q 10 8 5

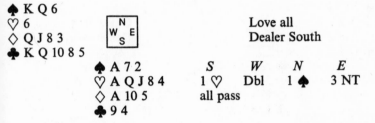

Love all
Dealer South

♠ A 7 2
♡ A Q J 8 4
◇ A 10 5
♣ 9 4

S	W	N	E
1 ♡	Dbl	1 ♠	3 NT
all pass			

On your lead of the queen of hearts North plays the two and East
the king. At trick two you capture the king of diamonds with your
ace. How do you continue?

Solution on page 90

Board 28

♠ Q 5
♡ Q 7 2
◇ K 9 8 5
♣ K 10 6 3

N-S game
Dealer West

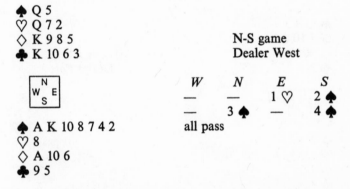

♠ A K 10 8 7 4 2
♡ 8
◇ A 10 6
♣ 9 5

W	N	E	S
—	—	1 ♡	2 ♠
—	3 ♠	—	4 ♠
all pass			

West leads the three of diamonds to the five, jack and ace. You
draw trumps in three rounds, throwing a club from dummy while
East discards two hearts. How should you continue?

Solution on page 92

Board 29

```
♠ 10 7 2
♡ A J 7 4          ┌─────┐         Game all
◇ A 8 2           │  N  │          Dealer North
♣ Q J 5           │W   E│
                  │  S  │
                  └─────┘
          ♠ A 5           W    N    E      S
          ♡ 3             —    1 ♡  2 ◇
          ◇ K J 10 9 6 3  3 ♡  —    4 ♡   all pass
          ♣ K 8 7 2
```

On your lead of the ace of spades North plays the nine and East the four. North wins the next spade with the king and returns the six. East follows suit with the jack and queen of spades, and you ruff with your lone trump. What do you lead to trick four?

Solution on page 94

Board 30

```
♠ Q 8 3
♡ J 10 6 2
◇ K 9 4 3                  Love all
♣ 8 4                      Dealer East

   ┌─────┐          W    N     E     S
   │  N  │                      —     2 NT
   │W   E│          —    3 ♣    —     3 ♡
   │  S  │          —    4 ♡    all pass
   └─────┘
♠ A K J 5
♡ K Q 8 4
◇ J 5
♣ A Q J
```

West leads the three of hearts to the nine and queen. When you continue trumps West takes his ace and leads a third trump, on which East discards the two of spades. Both defenders follow suit when you lead a spade to the queen. How should you continue?

Solution on page 96

Board 31

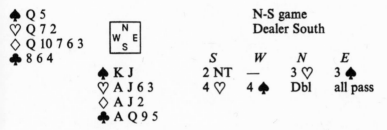

♠ Q 5
♡ Q 7 2
♢ Q 10 7 6 3
♣ 8 6 4

♠ K J
♡ A J 6 3
♢ A J 2
♣ A Q 9 5

N-S game
Dealer South

S	W	N	E
2 NT	—	3 ♡	3 ♠
4 ♡	4 ♠	Dbl	all pass

The ace of hearts wins the first trick, but East ruffs the next heart and leads a spade. You win with the king as North follows with the four. East ruffs a third heart and leads another spade to the queen, North completing an echo with the three. Then comes the three of diamonds, on which North plays the eight and East the king. How do you plan the defence?

Solution on page 98

Board 32

♠ K 6 3
♡ J 7 6 3
♢ A K Q 5
♣ 9 4

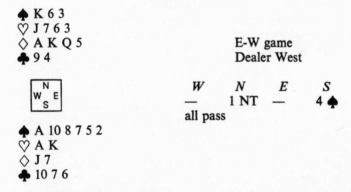

♠ A 10 8 7 5 2
♡ A K
♢ J 7
♣ 10 7 6

E-W game
Dealer West

W	N	E	S
—	1 NT	—	4 ♠
all pass			

West leads the king of clubs and continues with the queen. East overtakes with the ace and plays a third club, and you ruff the jack in dummy with the three of spades. How should you continue?

Solution on page 100

SOLUTIONS AND RESULTS

Board 25

PROBLEM

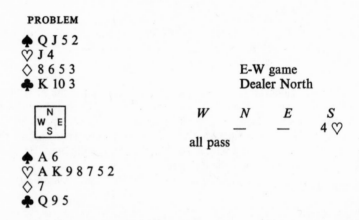

♠ Q J 5 2
♡ J 4
◇ 8 6 5 3
♣ K 10 3

E-W game
Dealer North

W	N	E	S
	—	—	4 ♡
all pass			

♠ A 6
♡ A K 9 8 7 5 2
◇ 7
♣ Q 9 5

On the lead of the ace of diamonds East drops the queen. West continues with the two of diamonds to his partner's ten. You ruff and cash the ace of hearts but the queen does not appear. When you continue with the king of hearts, West produces the queen and East the ten. What do you play now?

SOLUTION

There are nine certain tricks, and the tenth may come from a successful finesse in either clubs or spades. It may be difficult to find an entry in dummy, however, for you cannot count on either the ace or the jack of clubs being in the West hand.

In fact, if you are to avail yourself of the chances in both black suits there is only one way to play the clubs. At trick four you should lead the nine of clubs and run it. If this wins the trick or draws the ace, you have your tenth trick straight away. If the nine loses to the jack, you can make sure of an entry for the spade finesse by overtaking the queen of clubs with the king on the second round.

FULL HAND

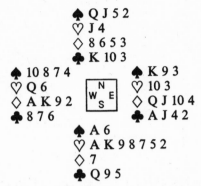

```
              ♠ Q J 5 2
              ♡ J 4
              ◇ 8 6 5 3
              ♣ K 10 3
♠ 10 8 7 4              ♠ K 9 3
♡ Q 6        N         ♡ 10 3
◇ A K 9 2  W   E       ◇ Q J 10 4
♣ 8 7 6        S       ♣ A J 4 2
              ♠ A 6
              ♡ A K 9 8 7 5 2
              ◇ 7
              ♣ Q 9 5
```

RESULT

In the other room South opened one heart and rebid three hearts
over his partner's response of one spade. There the bidding rested,
which was just as well from South's point of view since he made
only nine tricks. After drawing trumps he led the queen of clubs
from hand. East held up his ace, and the declarer could no longer
make a tenth trick.

Take 7 i.m.p. for tackling the clubs by running the nine. Anything
else loses 5 i.m.p.

Board 26

PROBLEM

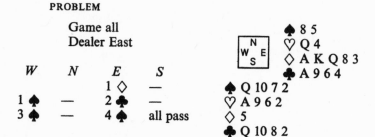

Game all
Dealer East

```
                          ♠ 8 5
                          ♡ Q 4
                          ◇ A K Q 8 3
                          ♣ A 9 6 4
W      N      E      S
              1◇     —      ♠ Q 10 7 2
1♠     —      2♣     —      ♡ A 9 6 2
3♠     —      4♠     all pass  ◇ 5
                          ♣ Q 10 8 2
```

North leads the five of hearts to your ace and wins the heart return with the king, West playing the seven and the ten. Winning the diamond switch with the ace, West leads a spade to his ace, regards North's nine with suspicion, and leads another diamond to the king. After ruffing, what do you return?

SOLUTION

West is marked with a six-card spade suit, and on the bidding he must surely have the king of clubs. If he has two clubs and three diamonds (unlikely in view of his play) he will always be able to make his contract by taking a spade finesse, but if he has three clubs and two diamonds the defence ought to prevail. Even if declarer has the jack of clubs as well as the king, he will be short of an entry in dummy and will be unable to finesse in both black suits. This presupposes, of course, that you do not solve declarer's problems for him by returning a spade or a club.

Only one other line of defence remains to be considered—a heart return, offering declarer a ruff and discard. This Greek gift may bring West a moment of pleasure but the pain will not be far behind. If he ruffs the heart in his own hand he will lack the entries to finesse in both black suits, while if he discards a club from hand and ruffs the heart on the table he will be unable to catch your queen of trumps. Nor will it help to ruff in both hands. The contract is bound to go down on a heart return.

FULL HAND

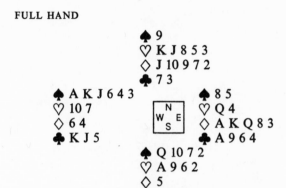

```
                    ♠ 9
                    ♡ K J 8 5 3
                    ◇ J 10 9 7 2
                    ♣ 7 3
  ♠ A K J 6 4 3            ♠ 8 5
  ♡ 10 7          N        ♡ Q 4
  ◇ 6 4        W   E       ◇ A K Q 8 3
  ♣ K J 5         S        ♣ A 9 6 4
                    ♠ Q 10 7 2
                    ♡ A 9 6 2
                    ◇ 5
                    ♣ Q 10 8 2
```

RESULT

In the other room the bidding and the early play followed the same course, but your team-mate in the West seat was not so careless as to attempt to enter dummy with a second diamond. He led a club to the ace, finessed in trumps, conceded a trump and claimed ten tricks.

A heart return is therefore worth 12 i.m.p. to your team, while anything else results in a flat board.

Board 27

PROBLEM

♠ K Q 6
♡ 6
◇ Q J 8 3
♣ K Q 10 8 5

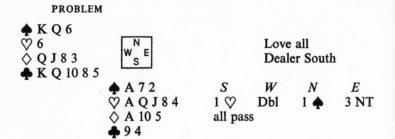

Love all
Dealer South

♠ A 7 2
♡ A Q J 8 4
◇ A 10 5
♣ 9 4

S	W	N	E
1 ♡	Dbl	1 ♠	3 NT
all pass			

On your lead of the queen of hearts North plays the two and East the king. At trick two you capture the king of diamonds with your ace. How do you continue?

SOLUTION

The critical point of the hand has now been reached. From declarer's failure to tackle clubs you can safely assume that he has five tricks in the suit. He has already made a heart trick, at least two tricks have been established in diamonds, and further tricks can be established in spades. Clearly declarer is likely to make his contract unless you can take enough tricks to defeat him right now.

Cashing the hearts from the top can be the winning defence only if North started with four cards in the suit. But that is surely not possible. With four hearts partner would have raised hearts rather than mention his spade suit. You are forced to the conclusion that the contract cannot be defeated unless partner has the ten of hearts, and you should therefore lead a small heart at trick three.

FULL HAND

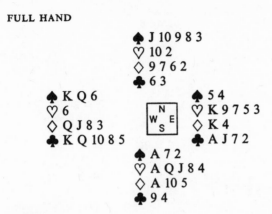

```
                    ♠ J 10 9 8 3
                    ♡ 10 2
                    ◇ 9 7 6 2
                    ♣ 6 3
   ♠ K Q 6                        ♠ 5 4
   ♡ 6              ┌─────┐       ♡ K 9 7 5 3
   ◇ Q J 8 3       │  N  │       ◇ K 4
   ♣ K Q 10 8 5    │W   E│       ♣ A J 7 2
                   │  S  │
                   └─────┘
                    ♠ A 7 2
                    ♡ A Q J 8 4
                    ◇ A 10 5
                    ♣ 9 4
```

RESULT

Against the same contract in the other room your opponents found the correct defence, so you can do no better than tie the board. The lead of anything but a small heart after winning the ace of diamonds costs 10 i.m.p.

Board 28

PROBLEM

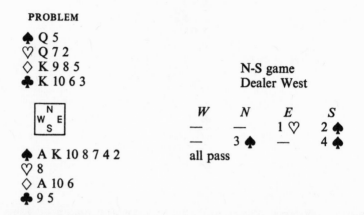

♠ Q 5
♡ Q 7 2
◇ K 9 8 5
♣ K 10 6 3

N-S game
Dealer West

♠ A K 10 8 7 4 2
♡ 8
◇ A 10 6
♣ 9 5

W	N	E	S
—	—	1 ♡	2 ♠
—	3 ♠	—	4 ♠
all pass			

West leads the three of diamonds to the five, jack and ace. You draw trumps in three rounds, throwing a club from dummy while East discards two hearts. How should you continue?

SOLUTION

There are nine top tricks, and at first glance it seems a matter of routine to establish the tenth in diamonds. Closer inspection may reveal the hidden danger. Running the ten of diamonds will certainly bring in an overtrick if the initial lead was from the queen, but there is no guarantee that this is the case. The three of diamonds may be a singleton, or even the top card of a doubleton. In that event, after winning the queen of diamonds, East may be able to put his partner on lead in hearts, and a club switch may set up four tricks for the defence.

To give yourself every chance, you should cut the defensive communications at this point by leading your heart. If East wins the trick, you will subsequently be able to run the ten of diamonds with complete safety.

If West is able to win the heart trick, your contract will still be safe unless East has all three club honours. On a heart or diamond return you can again duck a diamond to East. And on a club return you can play low from dummy, hoping to set up a club trick to take care of your losing diamond.

FULL HAND

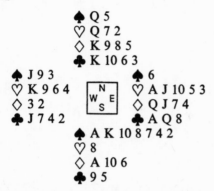

```
              ♠ Q 5
              ♡ Q 7 2
              ◇ K 9 8 5
              ♣ K 10 6 3
♠ J 9 3                      ♠ 6
♡ K 9 6 4         N         ♡ A J 10 5 3
◇ 3 2         W     E        ◇ Q J 7 4
♣ J 7 4 2         S         ♣ A Q 8
              ♠ A K 10 8 7 4 2
              ♡ 8
              ◇ A 10 6
              ♣ 9 5
```

RESULT

The contract was the same in the other room, and your team-mate in the West seat chose an unfortunate moment to have a look at dummy. He led the king of hearts and that was the end of the defence.

You therefore needed to find the scissors coup to earn a flat board. The lead of anything but the heart costs 12 i.m.p.

Board 29

PROBLEM

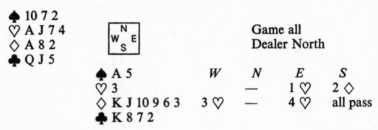

♠ 10 7 2
♡ A J 7 4
◇ A 8 2
♣ Q J 5

Game all
Dealer North

♠ A 5
♡ 3
◇ K J 10 9 6 3
♣ K 8 7 2

W	N	E	S
—	1 ♡	2 ◇
3 ♡	—	4 ♡	all pass

On your lead of the ace of spades North plays the nine and East the four. North wins the next spade with the king and returns the six. East follows suit with the jack and queen of spades, and you ruff with your lone trump. What do you lead to trick four?

SOLUTION

In a sense it is gratifying to have found the spade ruff, but you appear to have end-played yourself in the process. Declarer is sure to have the ace of clubs and he is quite likely to have the queen of diamonds, so that whatever you return may cost a trick. However, even if your return presents declarer with a third trick in the minor suits, he will need seven trumps to bring his total up to ten. If he has six trumps he will have no more than nine immediate tricks, although there is a danger that a minor suit squeeze will provide him with a tenth trick.

The ace of diamonds is the only entry to dummy, and you can kill all chance of this hypothetical squeeze by taking out that card. The correct lead at trick four is the king of diamonds.

FULL HAND

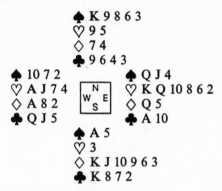

♠ K 9 8 6 3
♡ 9 5
◇ 7 4
♣ 9 6 4 3

♠ 10 7 2   ♠ Q J 4
♡ A J 7 4   ♡ K Q 10 8 6 2
◇ A 8 2   ◇ Q 5
♣ Q J 5   ♣ A 10

♠ A 5
♡ 3
◇ K J 10 9 6 3
♣ K 8 7 2

After the return of the king of diamonds the declarer has to pin his faith on the club finesse.

RESULT

In the other room, after an opening bid of one heart and an overcall of two diamonds, West bid three diamonds. This had the effect of steering his partner into an unassailable three no trumps. On a diamond lead East made ten tricks.

You therefore gain 12 i.m.p. if you found the switch to the king of diamonds at trick four. Otherwise it is a flat board.

Board 30

PROBLEM

♠ Q 8 3
♡ J 10 6 2
◇ K 9 4 3
♣ 8 4

Love all
Dealer East

```
      N
   W     E
      S
```

♠ A K J 5
♡ K Q 8 4
◇ J 5
♣ A Q J

W	*N*	*E*	*S*
		—	2 NT
—	3 ♣	—	3 ♡
—	4 ♡	all pass	

West leads the three of hearts to the nine and queen. When you continue trumps West takes his ace and leads a third trump, on which East discards the two of spades. Both defenders follow suit when you lead a spade to the queen. How should you continue?

SOLUTION

You note with regret that you are not in the best contract. We are so conditioned to seeking out the 4–4 major fit that we tend to play in it even when three no trumps is superior.

In four hearts your problem is to avoid losing three tricks in the minor suits. There are several ways of tackling the hand but only one that is completely safe. You should run the rest of the spades, discarding a club from the table, then cash the ace of clubs and lead a diamond from hand. It does not matter whether you lead the jack or the five. If you choose to lead the jack, you must run it to East unless West covers with the queen. If you lead the five, you should put in the nine from dummy unless West plays an honour card.

When East wins the trick, he will be compelled to yield your tenth trick whether he returns a diamond or a club.

FULL HAND

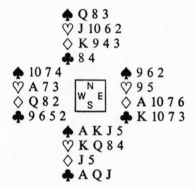

```
                    ♠ Q 8 3
                    ♡ J 10 6 2
                    ◇ K 9 4 3
                    ♣ 8 4
        ♠ 10 7 4              ♠ 9 6 2
        ♡ A 7 3      N        ♡ 9 5
        ◇ Q 8 2   W     E     ◇ A 10 7 6
        ♣ 9 6 5 2    S        ♣ K 10 7 3
                    ♠ A K J 5
                    ♡ K Q 8 4
                    ◇ J 5
                    ♣ A Q J
```

RESULT

There are times when virtue has to be its own reward. In the other room the contract was also four hearts, and declarer made ten tricks by taking a straightforward club finesse.

It is therefore a flat board if you made your contract by any method. It costs 10 i.m.p. if you went down.

D

Board 31

PROBLEM

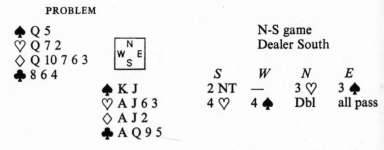

♠ Q 5
♡ Q 7 2
◇ Q 10 7 6 3
♣ 8 6 4

N-S game
Dealer South

♠ K J
♡ A J 6 3
◇ A J 2
♣ A Q 9 5

S	W	N	E
2 NT	—	3 ♡	3 ♠
4 ♡	4 ♠	Dbl	all pass

The ace of hearts wins the first trick, but East ruffs the next heart and leads a spade. You win with the king as North follows with the four. East ruffs a third heart and leads another spade to the queen, North completing an echo with the three. Then comes the three of diamonds, on which North plays the eight and East the king. How do you plan the defence?

SOLUTION

It is annoying when the opponents insist on sacrificing against your big hands, and it can be even more annoying if you fail to exact the maximum penalty.

On this hand partner's carding marks him with a third trump and a doubleton diamond, and it should be clear that you can engineer a ruff for him by winning the ace of diamonds at once and returning the jack of diamonds. The declarer is thus locked in dummy with no way of drawing the outstanding trump. You can win a club lead, give partner his diamond ruff, and subsequently score one or two further tricks in clubs.

FULL HAND

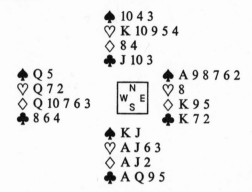

♠ 10 4 3
♡ K 10 9 5 4
◇ 8 4
♣ J 10 3

♠ Q 5
♡ Q 7 2
◇ Q 10 7 6 3
♣ 8 6 4

♠ A 9 8 7 6 2
♡ 8
◇ K 9 5
♣ K 7 2

♠ K J
♡ A J 6 3
◇ A J 2
♣ A Q 9 5

As you can see, the diamond ruff is needed to bring the penalty up to 700.

RESULT

In the other room your team-mates did not enter the bidding, and East led a diamond against four hearts. Declarer played the ace, cashed the ace and king of hearts, discarded his losing diamond on the fourth club after a successful finesse, and eventually misguessed the spades to make ten tricks.

You therefore gain 2 i.m.p. for achieving a penalty of 700, but you lose 3 i.m.p. if you held up the ace of diamonds until the third round. Winning the ace of diamonds and returning the two costs 11 i.m.p., as does returning a heart or cashing the ace of clubs. Taking the ace of diamonds and switching to a small club gives East his contract and costs 15 i.m.p.

Board 32

PROBLEM

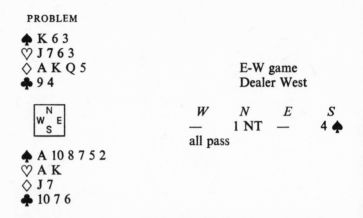

♠ K 6 3
♡ J 7 6 3
◇ A K Q 5
♣ 9 4

E-W game
Dealer West

♠ A 10 8 7 5 2
♡ A K
◇ J 7
♣ 10 7 6

W	N	E	S
—	1 NT	—	4 ♠
all pass			

West leads the king of clubs and continues with the queen. East overtakes with the ace and plays a third club, and you ruff the jack in dummy with the three of spades. How should you continue?

SOLUTION

The problem here is to avoid the loss of two trump tricks in the event of a bad break. If dummy's trumps had not been shortened, you would have had a simple safety play to cater for four trumps in the East hand. If West showed out on the lead of the king of spades and East failed to split his honours on the second round, you could finesse the ten. If East played an honour on the second round you could win, play three rounds of diamonds for a club discard, and lead the third trump from the table.

Now the situation is different. You will be poorly placed if you cash the king of spades and West shows out. East will certainly split his honours on the second round, and you will have no way of preventing him from scoring two trump tricks.

What is needed is an extra entry in dummy to enable you to bring off a trump coup if the dangerous situation exists. That extra entry may be found only by leaving the king of spades on the table. Lead the six of spades and insert the ten if East plays low. West will be able to do no damage if he can win the trick.

If East plays an honour to force your ace and West shows out, however, you can continue by cashing the top hearts, leading a diamond to dummy, ruffing a heart, returning in diamonds and ruffing another heart or a diamond. A trump to the king will then leave you in a position to score your tenth trick *en passant* with the ten of spades.

FULL HAND

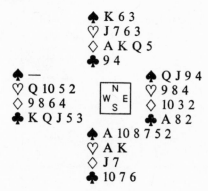

```
                    ♠ K 6 3
                    ♡ J 7 6 3
                    ◇ A K Q 5
                    ♣ 9 4
   ♠ —                            ♠ Q J 9 4
   ♡ Q 10 5 2          N          ♡ 9 8 4
   ◇ 9 8 6 4        W     E       ◇ 10 3 2
   ♣ K Q J 5 3         S          ♣ A 8 2
                    ♠ A 10 8 7 5 2
                    ♡ A K
                    ◇ J 7
                    ♣ 10 7 6
```

RESULT

The contract and the defence were the same at the other table, but declarer played the king of spades at trick four and went one down.

Take 10 i.m.p. if you found the play to make the contract.

SCORECARD

	Maximum Gain		Maximum Loss		Your Score	
B/F	+ 173	− 4	+ 6	− 162	+	−
Board 25	7			5		
26	12					
27				10		
28				12		
29	12					
30				10		
31	2			15		
32	10					
Total C/F	216	4	6	214		
Net Score	212			208		

The time is 4.25 and a fifteen-minute tea-break is scheduled. The afternoon sun slants through the windows of the lounge as you munch a cucumber sandwich and let the bridge talk flow around you. Idly you wonder why these hotels are always overheated, and why you seem to be getting all the problems at the table.

By now the captain appears to regard you and your partner as his anchor pair, and he asks if you are prepared to continue. Well, who would ask to be taken out? You swallow a second cup of tea and return to the arena for the next set of boards.

FIFTH SESSION

Boards 33 to 40

PROBLEMS

Board 33

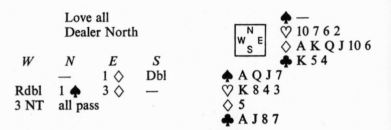

Love all
Dealer North

♠ —
♡ 10 7 6 2
◇ A K Q J 10 6
♣ K 5 4

W	N	E	S
—	1 ◇		Dbl
Rdbl	1 ♠	3 ◇	—
3 NT	all pass		

♠ A Q J 7
♡ K 8 4 3
◇ 5
♣ A J 8 7

North leads the ten of clubs which runs to declarer's queen. At trick two West leads a diamond to the table and continues diamonds, diamonds, diamonds. Plan your five discards.

Solution on page 108

Board 34

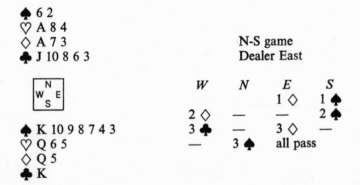

♠ 6 2
♡ A 8 4
◇ A 7 3
♣ J 10 8 6 3

N-S game
Dealer East

♠ K 10 9 8 7 4 3
♡ Q 6 5
◇ Q 5
♣ K

W	N	E	S
		1 ◇	1 ♠
2 ◇	—	—	2 ♠
3 ♣	—	3 ◇	—
—	3 ♠	all pass	

West leads the two of diamonds. When you play low from the table, East produces the king and returns the seven of clubs to his partner's ace. West switches back to the jack of diamonds. How do you play?

Solution on page 110

Board 35

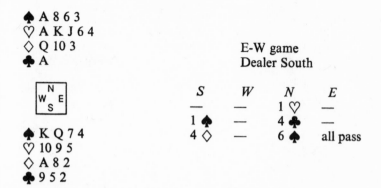

♠ A 8 6 3
♡ A K J 6 4
◇ Q 10 3
♣ A

E-W game
Dealer South

♠ K Q 7 4
♡ 10 9 5
◇ A 8 2
♣ 9 5 2

S	W	N	E
—	—	1 ♡	—
1 ♠	—	4 ♣	—
4 ◇	—	6 ♠	all pass

West leads the queen of clubs to dummy's ace. How do you plan the play?

Solution on page 112

Board 36

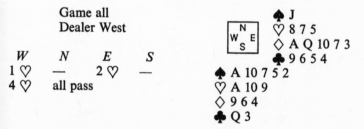

Game all
Dealer West

♠ J
♡ 8 7 5
◇ A Q 10 7 3
♣ 9 6 5 4

♠ A 10 7 5 2
♡ A 10 9
◇ 9 6 4
♣ Q 3

W	N	E	S
1 ♡	—	2 ♡	—
4 ♡	all pass		

North leads the nine of spades and West drops the four under your ace. At trick two you lead the queen of clubs, on which West plays the two and North the ten. When you continue with the three of clubs West plays the ace and North the jack. Declarer leads the king of hearts, North playing the two and you the nine. West continues with the queen of hearts on which North plays the six. How do you plan the defence?

Solution on page 114

Board 37

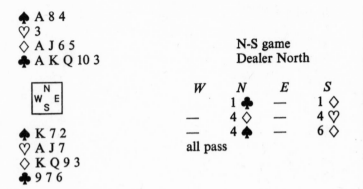

♠ A 8 4
♡ 3
♢ A J 6 5
♣ A K Q 10 3

N-S game
Dealer North

W	N	E	S
	1 ♣	—	1 ♢
—	4 ♢	—	4 ♡
—	4 ♠	—	6 ♢
all pass			

♠ K 7 2
♡ A J 7
♢ K Q 9 3
♣ 9 7 6

West leads the nine of hearts to the queen and ace. How do you plan the play?

Solution on page 116

Board 38

E-W game
Dealer East

♠ 10 6 3
♡ K Q 7 5 4 3
♢ K 5
♣ Q 6

W	N	E	S
		1 ♣	1 ♢
1 ♡	—	1 NT*	—
3 ♡	—	3 NT	all pass

♠ A K J 4
♡ 9 8
♢ Q J 9 7 6 3
♣ 10

15–16 points

On your lead of the king of spades North plays the five and East the eight. How should you continue?

Solution on page 118

Board 39

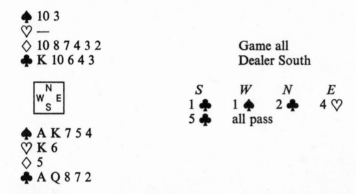

♠ 10 3
♡ —
♢ 10 8 7 4 3 2
♣ K 10 6 4 3

Game all
Dealer South

♠ A K 7 5 4
♡ K 6
♢ 5
♣ A Q 8 7 2

S	W	N	E
1 ♣	1 ♠	2 ♣	4 ♡
5 ♣	all pass		

West leads the jack of clubs, East contributes the five, and you win with the queen. When you lead the five of diamonds West plays the jack, but East overtakes with the queen and returns the nine of clubs. You play low from hand and win in dummy, while West discards the ten of hearts. On the lead of a diamond from the table East discards a heart and you ruff. How should you continue?

Solution on page 120

Board 40

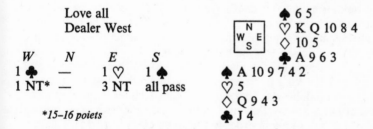

Love all
Dealer West

♠ 6 5
♡ K Q 10 8 4
♢ 10 5
♣ A 9 6 3

♠ A 10 9 7 4 2
♡ 5
♢ Q 9 4 3
♣ J 4

W	N	E	S
1 ♣	—	1 ♡	1 ♠
1 NT*	—	3 NT	all pass

*15–16 poiets

North leads the eight of spades. How do you plan to defeat the contract?

Solution on page 122

SOLUTIONS AND RESULTS

Board 33

Love all
Dealer North

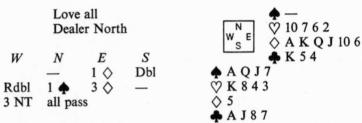

♠ —
♡ 10 7 6 2
◇ A K Q J 10 6
♣ K 5 4

W	N	E	S
—	1 ◇	Dbl	
Rdbl	1 ♠	3 ◇	—
3 NT	all pass		

♠ A Q J 7
♡ K 8 4 3
◇ 5
♣ A J 8 7

North leads the ten of clubs which runs to declarer's queen. At trick two West leads a diamond to the table and continues diamonds, diamonds, diamonds. Plan your five discards.

SOLUTION

Declarer has six diamond tricks on view, he has already made a club trick, and he therefore needs two heart tricks for his contract. If he has both ace and queen of hearts he will make nine tricks with the aid of the finesse.

Looking at it from another angle, what is needed to defeat the contract is a further club lead from North. That will be possible only if partner has the queen of hearts, and you should therefore defend on the assumption that he has that card.

Your discards on the diamonds should be three spades, a small heart and the king of hearts. Do not make the mistake of parting with two small hearts. That would enable declarer to develop at least nine tricks without allowing North to gain the lead. You must get rid of the heart king in order to create an entry in partner's hand.

FULL HAND

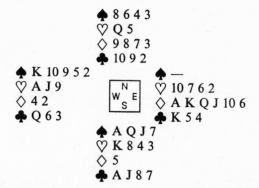

♠ 8 6 4 3
♡ Q 5
♢ 9 8 7 3
♣ 10 9 2

♠ K 10 9 5 2
♡ A J 9
♢ 4 2
♣ Q 6 3

♠ —
♡ 10 7 6 2
♢ A K Q J 10 6
♣ K 5 4

♠ A Q J 7
♡ K 8 4 3
♢ 5
♣ A J 8 7

You can see what happens if you keep the king and another heart in your hand. A heart is led from dummy. If you play low, West plays the ace and another heart to put you in, while if you play the king you are allowed to hold the trick. In either case declarer makes ten tricks.

RESULT

Disaster! In the other room your team-mates doubled South in two spades, and he managed to scramble home with eight tricks for a score of 470.

You lose 9 i.m.p. if you *kept* two small hearts in your hand, and you lose 14 if you *discarded* two small hearts.

Board 34

PROBLEM

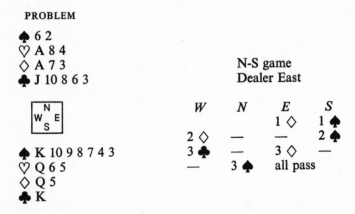

♠ 6 2
♡ A 8 4
◇ A 7 3
♣ J 10 8 6 3

N-S game
Dealer East

♠ K 10 9 8 7 4 3
♡ Q 6 5
◇ Q 5
♣ K

W	N	E	S
		1 ◇	1 ♠
2 ◇	—	—	2 ♠
3 ♣	—	3 ◇	—
—	3 ♠	all pass	

West leads the two of diamonds. When you play low from the table, East produces the king and returns the seven of clubs to his partner's ace. West switches back to the jack of diamonds. How do you play?

SOLUTION

With a loser in each of the side suits, you need to avoid the loss of more than one trump if you are to make this contract. In practice that means playing for East to have the ace and one other trump.

It is tempting to win this trick with the queen of diamonds, cross to the ace of hearts, discard a heart on the ace of diamonds and then lead a trump, but that is the road to certain defeat. East will rise with the ace of trumps, cash the king of hearts (which he surely must have on the bidding), and lead a diamond to promote a second trump trick for the defence.

To avert the threat of this trump promotion you must go up with the ace of diamonds on the second round and lead a trump. After ruffing the club or diamond return, you can draw the outstanding trumps, lead a heart to the ace and return a heart towards your queen.

FULL HAND

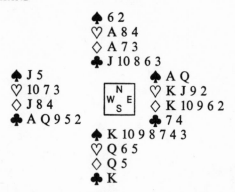

```
                  ♠ 6 2
                  ♡ A 8 4
                  ◇ A 7 3
                  ♣ J 10 8 6 3
   ♠ J 5                          ♠ A Q
   ♡ 10 7 3          N            ♡ K J 9 2
   ◇ J 8 4        W     E         ◇ K 10 9 6 2
   ♣ A Q 9 5 2       S            ♣ 7 4
                  ♠ K 10 9 8 7 4 3
                  ♡ Q 6 5
                  ◇ Q 5
                  ♣ K
```

RESULT

In the other room your team-mates played in three diamonds and made nine tricks on a friendly spade lead.

Making three spades is therefore worth 6 i.m.p. to your team. It is a flat board if you failed.

Board 35

PROBLEM

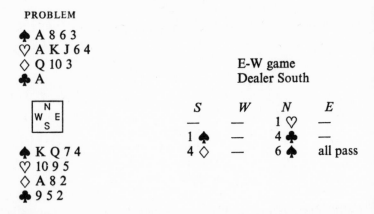

♠ A 8 6 3
♡ A K J 6 4
◇ Q 10 3
♣ A

E-W game
Dealer South

	S	W	N	E
	—	—	1 ♡	—
	1 ♠	—	4 ♣	—
	4 ◇	—	6 ♠	all pass

♠ K Q 7 4
♡ 10 9 5
◇ A 8 2
♣ 9 5 2

West leads the queen of clubs to dummy's ace. How do you plan the play?

SOLUTION

Partner's aggressive bidding has propelled you into a distinctly poor slam. At first glance it looks as though you need the heart finesse as well as a 3–2 trump break, giving you a chance of no more than 34 per cent.

However, if you can manage to ruff two clubs in dummy you will no longer be dependent on the heart finesse. You are short of an entry in your own hand, but if the hearts are 3–2 you can create an extra entry by leading a low heart to your nine at trick two. You will be able to win a diamond return with the ace, ruff a club, play the ace of spades and a spade to your king, and ruff another club. The ten of hearts will serve as the extra entry needed to draw the last trump, and your losing diamonds will go away on the hearts.

This line of play offers a better chance than the heart finesse, raising your expectancy of success to 46 per cent.

FULL HAND

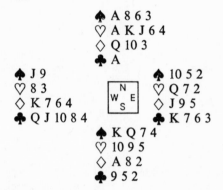

♠ A 8 6 3
♡ A K J 6 4
◇ Q 10 3
♣ A

♠ J 9   ♠ 10 5 2
♡ 8 3   ♡ Q 7 2
◇ K 7 6 4   ◇ J 9 5
♣ Q J 10 8 4   ♣ K 7 6 3

♠ K Q 7 4
♡ 10 9 5
◇ A 8 2
♣ 9 5 2

RESULT

In the other room, as expected, your opponents were quite content to play in four spades. They made eleven tricks for a score of 450.

Making the slam is therefore worth 11 i.m.p. to your team, while going down costs a like amount.

Board 36

Game all
Dealer West

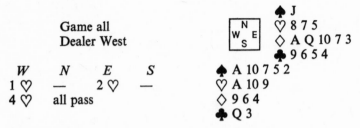

♠ J
♥ 8 7 5
♦ A Q 10 7 3
♣ 9 6 5 4

♠ A 10 7 5 2
♥ A 10 9
♦ 9 6 4
♣ Q 3

W	N	E	S
1 ♥	—	2 ♥	—
4 ♥	all pass		

North leads the nine of spades and West drops the four under your ace. At trick two you lead the queen of clubs, on which West plays the two and North the ten. When you continue with the three of clubs West plays the ace and North the jack. Declarer leads the king of hearts, North playing the two and you the nine. West continues with the queen of hearts on which North plays the six. How do you plan the defence?

By this stage a complete picture of declarer's hand is available. Since West has made no attempt to ruff a spade in dummy, his holding in the suit must be precisely K Q 4. He has five hearts headed by K Q J, four clubs headed by the ace, and therefore a singleton diamond. Even with the help of the diamond finesse he has only nine tricks.

Naturally you must win the second trump, otherwise declarer will discard dummy's clubs on his master spades and ruff out the king of clubs. A passive return of a spade or a trump will not be good enough, however. On the run of the trumps and the spades North would then be squeezed in the minor suits and West would make ten tricks after all.

The correct defence after winning the ace of hearts is to switch to a diamond. This cuts declarer's link with dummy and breaks up the threatening squeeze.

FULL HAND

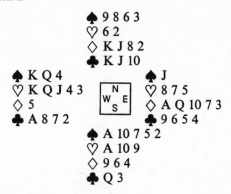

```
                 ♠ 9 8 6 3
                 ♡ 6 2
                 ◇ K J 8 2
                 ♣ K J 10
   ♠ K Q 4                    ♠ J
   ♡ K Q J 4 3      N         ♡ 8 7 5
   ◇ 5           W     E      ◇ A Q 10 7 3
   ♣ A 8 7 2        S         ♣ 9 6 5 4
                 ♠ A 10 7 5 2
                 ♡ A 10 9
                 ◇ 9 6 4
                 ♣ Q 3
```

RESULT

In the other room your team-mates also reached this thin game. The optimum defence was not found and your side scored 620.

Take a well-deserved 12 i.m.p. for finding the diamond switch. Anything else gives you a flat board.

Board 37

PROBLEM

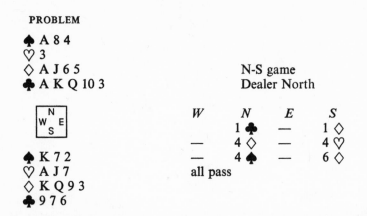

♠ A 8 4
♡ 3
◇ A J 6 5
♣ A K Q 10 3

N-S game
Dealer North

♠ K 7 2
♡ A J 7
◇ K Q 9 3
♣ 9 7 6

W	N	E	S
	1 ♣	—	1 ◇
—	4 ◇	—	4 ♡
—	4 ♠	—	6 ◇
all pass			

West leads the nine of hearts to the queen and ace. How do you plan the play?

SOLUTION

This time it looks as though you may have underbid the hand. Normal breaks in the minor suits will certainly produce thirteen tricks. It is therefore a suitable occasion for trying to protect yourself against bad breaks.

Suppose you ruff a heart at trick two, then cash the ace of diamonds and return the six of diamonds to your king. If diamonds are 3–2 you will be able to ruff the other heart loser, return to the king of spades, draw the last trump, and make your contract irrespective of the club division. But if the trumps are 4–1 this line will leave you dependent on a 3–2 club break.

With the position of the king of hearts marked on your right, however, it should be possible to cater for 4–1 breaks in both minor suits. Just ruff the small heart in dummy and continue with the ace, jack and another trump, drawing the fourth round if necessary. Then test the clubs by playing the ace and king. If East shows out, return to the king of spades and take the marked club finesse for thirteen tricks.

If it is West who shows out on the second club, the play of the ace of spades followed by the king will force East to bare his king of hearts. He can then be thrown in with the heart to lead into the club tenace.

FULL HAND

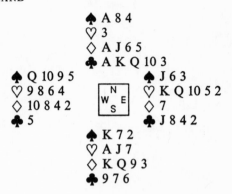

```
              ♠ A 8 4
              ♡ 3
              ◇ A J 6 5
              ♣ A K Q 10 3
♠ Q 10 9 5                    ♠ J 6 3
♡ 9 8 6 4         N          ♡ K Q 10 5 2
◇ 10 8 4 2     W     E        ◇ 7
♣ 5              S            ♣ J 8 4 2
              ♠ K 7 2
              ♡ A J 7
              ◇ K Q 9 3
              ♣ 9 7 6
```

RESULT

In the other room North played in six clubs on the lead of the king of hearts. As the cards lay, he was unable to avoid the loss of two tricks.

Making your slam is therefore worth 16 i.m.p.

Board 38

PROBLEM

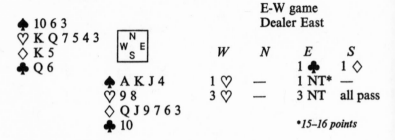

♠ 10 6 3
♡ K Q 7 5 4 3
◇ K 5
♣ Q 6

♠ A K J 4
♡ 9 8
◇ Q J 9 7 6 3
♣ 10

E-W game
Dealer East

W	N	E	S
		1 ♣	1 ◇
1 ♡	—	1 NT*	—
3 ♡	—	3 NT	all pass

•15–16 points

On your lead of the king of spades North plays the five and East the eight. How should you continue?

SOLUTION

Someone has started an echo in spades, but in the light of the bidding it is unlikely to be partner. It looks as though you ought to switch in an attempt to find partner's card of entry. If declarer has 15 points there is just room for partner to hold an ace.

The danger is that if you switch to the wrong suit declarer may be able to run six tricks in it, in which case you will come under in-tolerable pressure. Compelled to keep three diamonds, you will have to either shed a spade or void yourself in the other suits. No matter which course you choose declarer will be able to score a ninth trick.

Should you switch to a heart or a club? To come up with the right answer you must again consider the bidding. East has a tenuous holding in spades and only one diamond stopper, yet he preferred three no trumps to four hearts. Surely he can have no more than one heart. If that is the case, a heart switch cannot cost the contract even if declarer has the singleton ace.

You should therefore lead the nine of hearts at trick two.

FULL HAND

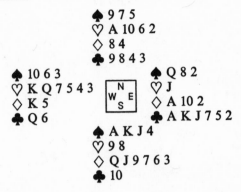

```
              ♠ 9 7 5
              ♡ A 10 6 2
              ◇ 8 4
              ♣ 9 8 4 3
♠ 10 6 3                    ♠ Q 8 2
♡ K Q 7 5 4 3    N         ♡ J
◇ K 5          W   E       ◇ A 10 2
♣ Q 6            S         ♣ A K J 7 5 2
              ♠ A K J 4
              ♡ 9 8
              ◇ Q J 9 7 6 3
              ♣ 10
```

Note that either a diamond or a club switch is fatal.

RESULT

In the other room your team-mates played in a quiet three clubs, scoring 110. A heart switch at trick two therefore gains 6 i.m.p., while anything else loses 10.

Board 39

PROBLEM

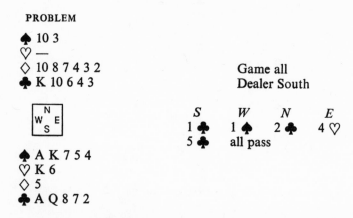

♠ 10 3
♡ —
♢ 10 8 7 4 3 2
♣ K 10 6 4 3

Game all
Dealer South

♠ A K 7 5 4
♡ K 6
♢ 5
♣ A Q 8 7 2

S	W	N	E
1♣	1♠	2♣	4♡
5♣	all pass		

West leads the jack of clubs, East contributes the five, and you win with the queen. When you lead the five of diamonds West plays the jack, but East overtakes with the queen and returns the nine of clubs. You play low from hand and win in dummy, while West discards the ten of hearts. On the lead of a diamond from the table East discards a heart and you ruff. How should you continue?

SOLUTION

Those trump leads by the defenders were far from friendly. Even so, it would have been an easy matter to make the contract with an overtrick but for the diabolical diamond break. Now it appears to be impossible to establish either the diamonds or the spades, and a cross-ruff will leave you a trick short of your contract.

Since West is known to have started with five diamonds as well as at least five spades, however, there should be a chance of a ruffing squeeze. In order to get the timing right you will need to concede a second trick, and you must concede it to East since you cannot stand a further diamond force at this point.

The correct move is to lead the king of hearts and pass it to East, discarding a diamond from the table. When your second heart is ruffed in dummy West will find the pressure too much for him. You will be able to establish your eleventh trick either in spades or in diamonds according to his discard.

FULL HAND

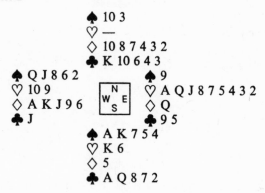

```
                    ♠ 10 3
                    ♡ —
                    ◇ 10 8 7 4 3 2
                    ♣ K 10 6 4 3
  ♠ Q J 8 6 2               ♠ 9
  ♡ 10 9          N         ♡ A Q J 8 7 5 4 3 2
  ◇ A K J 9 6   W   E       ◇ Q
  ♣ J              S        ♣ 9 5
                    ♠ A K 7 5 4
                    ♡ K 6
                    ◇ 5
                    ♣ A Q 8 7 2
```

RESULT

In the other room your team-mates sacrificed in five hearts doubled, escaping for one off at a cost of 200.

Making five clubs is therefore worth 9 i.m.p., while going one down loses 7 i.m.p.

Board 40

PROBLEM

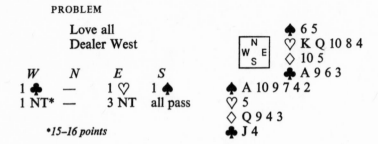

Love all
Dealer West

♠ 6 5
♡ K Q 10 8 4
◇ 10 5
♣ A 9 6 3

W	*N*	*E*	*S*
1 ♣	—	1 ♡	1 ♠
1 NT*	—	3 NT	all pass

♠ A 10 9 7 4 2
♡ 5
◇ Q 9 4 3
♣ J 4

•15–16 points

North leads the eight of spades. How do you plan to defeat the contract?

SOLUTION

The lead marks the king, queen and jack of spades in declarer's hand, and your own lack of entries means that you have to abandon all hope of establishing the suit. The only other possible source of nourishment for the defence is the diamond suit. It must be correct to take your ace of spades at trick one and switch to a diamond.

There remains the question of which card to lead. Partner will need to have four diamonds to give the defence a chance. One favourable possibility is that he has four diamonds headed by the king and jack plus the ace of hearts. If that is the position it will not matter which diamond you lead at trick two.

Alternatively, partner may have four diamonds headed by the ace and jack, with perhaps the queen of clubs on the side. To cater for this possibility as well as the first one, you should switch to the queen of diamonds at trick two.

FULL HAND

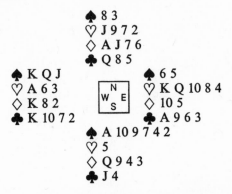

```
                    ♠ 8 3
                    ♡ J 9 7 2
                    ◇ A J 7 6
                    ♣ Q 8 5
    ♠ K Q J                      ♠ 6 5
    ♡ A 6 3          N           ♡ K Q 10 8 4
    ◇ K 8 2       W     E        ◇ 10 5
    ♣ K 10 7 2       S           ♣ A 9 6 3
                    ♠ A 10 9 7 4 2
                    ♡ 5
                    ◇ Q 9 4 3
                    ♣ J 4
```

As you can see, the lead of the queen of diamonds enables you to roll up the suit and put the contract one down.

RESULT

Your team-mates played in four hearts in the other room and the defenders made no mistake. South led a small diamond to his partner's jack. North returned a spade to the ace, and South led the queen of diamonds to pin the ten. East ruffed the third diamond, but eventually had to lose a club trick for one down.

You needed to find the switch to the queen of diamonds to tie the board. Allowing three no trumps to make costs 10 i.m.p.

SCORECARD

	Maximum Gain		Maximum Loss		Your Score	
	+	—	+	—	+	—
B/F	216	4	6	214		
Board 33		9		14		
34	6					
35	11			11		
36	12					
37	16					
38	6			10		
39	9			7		
40				10		
Total C/F	276	13	6	266		
Net Score	263			260		

After forty boards and forty problems you are beginning to feel the strain, but your captain decides to rest the pair who had the disaster on Board 33.

The time is 5.45 as you return to the table for the next set of boards.

SIXTH SESSION

Boards 41 to 48

PROBLEMS

Board 41

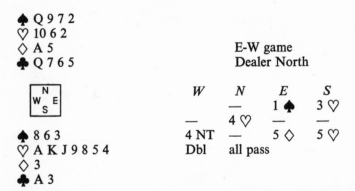

♠ Q 9 7 2
♡ 10 6 2
◇ A 5
♣ Q 7 6 5

E-W game
Dealer North

♠ 8 6 3
♡ A K J 9 8 5 4
◇ 3
♣ A 3

W	N	E	S
	—	1 ♠	3 ♡
—	4 ♡	—	—
4 NT	—	5 ◇	5 ♡
Dbl	all pass		

The four no trump bid is explained as showing length in both minor suits. West leads the queen of diamonds. How do you plan the play?

Solution on page 130

Board 42

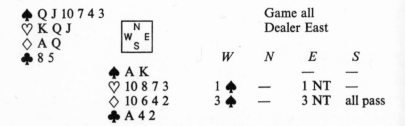

♠ Q J 10 7 4 3
♡ K Q J
◇ A Q
♣ 8 5

Game all
Dealer East

♠ A K
♡ 10 8 7 3
◇ 10 6 4 2
♣ A 4 2

W	N	E	S
		—	—
1 ♠	—	1 NT	—
3 ♠	—	3 NT	all pass

On your lead of the three of hearts dummy plays the jack, North the four and East the ace. East leads the nine of spades and partner drops the five under your king. You switch to the two of diamonds, and when the queen is played from dummy North produces the king. North returns the three of clubs and you capture the jack with your ace. How should you continue?

Solution on page 132

Board 43

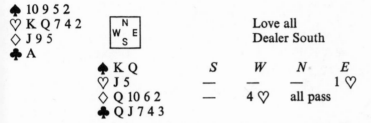

♠ 10 9 5 2
♡ K Q 7 4 2
◇ J 9 5
♣ A

Love all
Dealer South

♠ K Q
♡ J 5
◇ Q 10 6 2
♣ Q J 7 4 3

S	W	N	E
—	—	—	1 ♡
—	4 ♡	all pass	

On your lead of the king of spades partner plays the eight and declarer the three. You continue with the queen of spades, North playing the four and East the six. What now?

Solution on page 134

Board 44

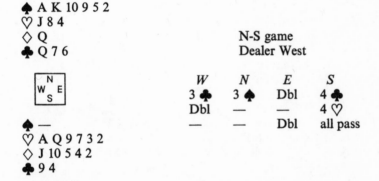

♠ A K 10 9 5 2
♡ J 8 4
◇ Q
♣ Q 7 6

N-S game
Dealer West

♠ —
♡ A Q 9 7 3 2
◇ J 10 5 4 2
♣ 9 4

W	N	E	S
3 ♣	3 ♠	Dbl	4 ♣
Dbl	—	—	4 ♡
—	—	Dbl	all pass

West leads the ace of clubs, dropping his partner's king. You cover the continuation of the jack of clubs with the queen, and East ruffs with the six of hearts. The return of the ten of hearts is won by dummy's jack, West following suit with the five. How should you continue?

Solution on page 136

Board 45

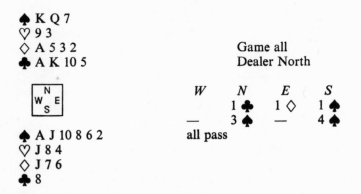

♠ K Q 7
♡ 9 3
◇ A 5 3 2
♣ A K 10 5

Game all
Dealer North

♠ A J 10 8 6 2
♡ J 8 4
◇ J 7 6
♣ 8

W	N	E	S
	1 ♣	1 ◇	1 ♠
—	3 ♣	—	4 ♠
all pass			

West leads the four of diamonds and you win the first trick with the ace. The play of the ace and king of clubs enables you to discard a losing diamond from hand. How should you continue?

Solution on page 138

Board 46

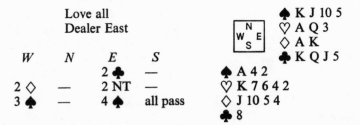

Love all
Dealer East

♠ K J 10 5
♡ A Q 3
◇ A K
♣ K Q J 5

♠ A 4 2
♡ K 7 6 4 2
◇ J 10 5 4
♣ 8

W	N	E	S
		2 ♣	—
2 ◇	—	2 NT	—
3 ♠	—	4 ♠	all pass

North leads the nine of hearts. The three is played from dummy, you win with the king and West plays the ten. Which card do you play at trick two?

Solution on page 140

Board 47

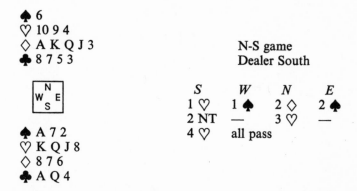

♠ 6
♡ 10 9 4
◇ A K Q J 3
♣ 8 7 5 3

N-S game
Dealer South

♠ A 7 2
♡ K Q J 8
◇ 8 7 6
♣ A Q 4

S	W	N	E
1 ♡	1 ♠	2 ◇	2 ♠
2 NT	—	3 ♡	—
4 ♡	all pass		

West leads the king of spades on which East plays the five. How do you plan the play?

Solution on page 142

Board 48

E-W game
Dealer West

♠ 9 7 3
♡ A 10 5
◇ 9 8 6 2
♣ K 7 5

♠ 8 6 2
♡ 8 7 4
◇ Q 5 3
♣ A Q 10 4

W	N	E	S
2 NT	—	3 NT	all pass

North leads the three of hearts to the five, seven and king. West leads the two of clubs, North plays the three and dummy the king. You win with the ace and switch to the eight of spades, on which West plays the queen. North wins with the king and returns the four of spades to declarer's ace. West continues with the jack of clubs, on which North discards the two of hearts. How do you play?

Solution on page 144

E

SOLUTIONS AND RESULTS

Board 41

PROBLEM

♠ Q 9 7 2
♡ 10 6 2
◇ A 5
♣ Q 7 6 5

E-W game
Dealer North

```
    N
  W   E
    S
```

♠ 8 6 3
♡ A K J 9 8 5 4
◇ 3
♣ A 3

W	N	E	S
—	—	1 ♠	3 ♡
—	4 ♡	—	—
4 NT	—	5 ◇	5 ♡
Dbl	all pass		

The four no trump bid is explained as showing length in both minor suits. West leads the queen of diamonds. How do you plan the play?

SOLUTION

No doubt you are wishing you had allowed the opponents to play in five diamonds. In five hearts you appear to have four losers in the black suits quite apart from a possible trump loser.

If there *is* a trump loser, five diamonds is probably on and your result should not be too bad. It is when the trumps are 2–1 that you need to make your doubled contract.

The one ray of hope is the absence of a spade lead, which may mean that West is void in the suit. In that case you should be able to get rid of one of your spade losers on the queen of clubs, since West is marked with length (and presumably strength) in the suit. And an end-play may provide your eleventh trick if you get the timing right.

The key play, after winning the first trick with the ace of diamonds, is to ruff the five of diamonds in hand. Then play the ace and king of hearts followed by the ace and another club. West will take his king and return a club to dummy's queen. You can discard a spade on this trick, and a further spade on the fourth round of clubs. With only minor suit cards left, West will have to give you a ruff and discard, enabling you to throw the last losing spade from your hand while ruffing in dummy.

FULL HAND

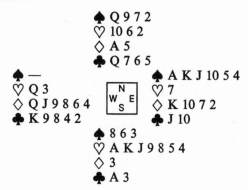

```
                    ♠ Q 9 7 2
                    ♡ 10 6 2
                    ◇ A 5
                    ♣ Q 7 6 5
    ♠ —                          ♠ A K J 10 5 4
    ♡ Q 3              N          ♡ 7
    ◇ Q J 9 8 6 4   W   E        ◇ K 10 7 2
    ♣ K 9 8 4 2        S         ♣ J 10
                    ♠ 8 6 3
                    ♡ A K J 9 8 5 4
                    ◇ 3
                    ♣ A 3
```

RESULT

In the other room your team-mates played in five diamonds doubled, losing the obvious three tricks and 200 points.

Five hearts doubled is worth 650, so take 10 i.m.p. if you made your contract. You lose 7 i.m.p. if you went one down, and 11 i.m.p. if you went two down.

Board 42

PROBLEM

♠ Q J 10 7 4 3
♡ K Q J
◇ A Q
♣ 8 5

```
      N
   W     E
      S
```

♠ A K
♡ 10 8 7 3
◇ 10 6 4 2
♣ A 4 2

Game all
Dealer East

W	N	E	S
		—	—
1 ♠	—	1 NT	—
3 ♠	—	3 NT	all pass

On your lead of the three of hearts dummy plays the jack, North the four and East the ace. East leads the nine of spades and partner drops the five under your king. You switch to the two of diamonds, and when the queen is played from dummy North produces the king. North returns the three of clubs and you capture the jack with your ace. How should you continue?

SOLUTION

The ace of spades represents a fourth trick for the defence, and a fifth can come only from clubs or diamonds. Which horse do you choose to back?

There is just room for partner to have the king of clubs, but in that case it does not matter what you return. With no way back to hand declarer must go one down. What other club holding could partner have? With Q 10 9 3 he would have led the ten rather than the three, so you can rule that out. A club return is needed if partner has led from Q 10 7 3 or Q 10 6 3, or even Q 10 3. But in that case declarer has played incorrectly. With K J 9 and one or two small cards, his proper play would be a low card in the hope that your partner has both the queen and the ten. Playing the jack would give him very little chance.

Don't insult declarer by assuming he has played badly. The odds are heavy that he has the ten of clubs to back up his jack, and you should therefore switch back to diamonds.

FULL HAND

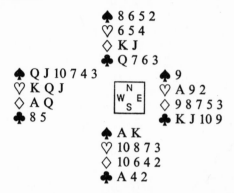

                 ♠ 8 6 5 2
                 ♡ 6 5 4
                 ◇ K J
                 ♣ Q 7 6 3

♠ Q J 10 7 4 3   ♠ 9
♡ K Q J   ♡ A 9 2
◇ A Q   ◇ 9 8 7 5 3
♣ 8 5   ♣ K J 10 9

                 ♠ A K
                 ♡ 10 8 7 3
                 ◇ 10 6 4 2
                 ♣ A 4 2

Partner could have saved you a headache by returning the jack of diamonds. His club return was correct, however. The club switch is vital if you have the king of clubs instead of the ace.

RESULT

In the other room your team-mates played in four spades, and a heart lead offered declarer some hope. West won in hand and led a club to the nine, which held the trick. Returning to hand with a second heart, he led another club to the ten. South took his ace and switched to diamonds. West went up with the ace, crossed to the ace of hearts, and discarded the queen of diamonds on the king of clubs. When he led a trump, however, South won and produced the thirteenth heart, thereby establishing a third trump trick for the defence.

It is therefore a flat board if you switched back to diamonds when in with the ace of clubs. You lose 12 i.m.p. if you led anything else.

Board 43

PROBLEM

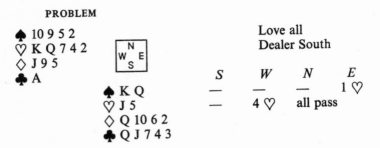

♠ 10 9 5 2
♡ K Q 7 4 2
◇ J 9 5
♣ A

Love all
Dealer South

♠ K Q
♡ J 5
◇ Q 10 6 2
♣ Q J 7 4 3

S	W	N	E
—	—	—	1 ♡
—	4 ♡	all pass	

On your lead of the king of spades partner plays the eight and declarer the three. You continue with the queen of spades, North playing the four and East the six. What now?

SOLUTION

You must hope that declarer has another spade loser, but partner will also need to have a high card in one of the red suits if the defence is to have a chance. In the unlikely event of partner having the ace of hearts you have nothing to worry about, for a spade ruff will always give you a fourth trick.

Partner's high card is more likely to be in diamonds, however. In that case you cannot afford to play a passive game. Suppose declarer has ace and another diamond and three spades headed by the jack. On a passive trump or club return he will draw trumps and lead the jack of spades, and his losing diamond will eventually be discarded on dummy's fourth spade.

The lead of a low diamond is likely to fare no better. The nine will draw partner's king and declarer will win with the ace. After drawing trumps he will return his second diamond, and his losing spade will disappear on the jack of diamonds.

You need to establish a diamond trick for partner rather than for yourself, and the correct move is to lead the queen of diamonds at trick three. This will render declarer helpless if he has the critical holding of three spades to the jack and ace and another diamond. Whether he wins or ducks he will be unable to prevent the defence from scoring four tricks.

FULL HAND

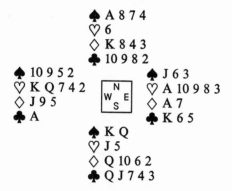

♠ A 8 7 4
♡ 6
◇ K 8 4 3
♣ 10 9 8 2

♠ 10 9 5 2   ♠ J 6 3
♡ K Q 7 4 2   ♡ A 10 9 8 3
◇ J 9 5   ◇ A 7
♣ A   ♣ K 6 5

♠ K Q
♡ J 5
◇ Q 10 6 2
♣ Q J 7 4 3

If you work it out you will realize that the switch to the queen of diamonds can never lose.

RESULT

Your team-mates also played in four hearts and South failed to find the killing defence.

Take 10 i.m.p. if you led the queen of diamonds at trick three. Otherwise it is a flat board.

Board 44

PROBLEM

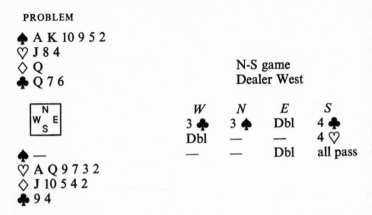

♠ A K 10 9 5 2
♡ J 8 4
◇ Q
♣ Q 7 6

N-S game
Dealer West

♠ —
♡ A Q 9 7 3 2
◇ J 10 5 4 2
♣ 9 4

W	N	E	S
3 ♣	3 ♠	Dbl	4 ♣
Dbl	—	—	4 ♡
—	—	Dbl	all pass

West leads the ace of clubs, dropping his partner's king. You cover the continuation of the jack of clubs with the queen, and East ruffs with the six of hearts. The return of the ten of hearts is won by dummy's jack, West following suit with the five. How should you continue?

SOLUTION

It seems that you may be able to teach East a sharp lesson here. Two of your diamonds can be discarded on the top spades, and if you can manage to ruff two more in dummy you will have ten tricks.

But will it be possible to ruff two diamonds in dummy? The bidding marks East with both ace and king, and when he wins the first diamond he will return the king of trumps, restricting you to one diamond ruff and nine tricks altogether.

It cannot be right, in that case, to lead the queen of diamonds at trick four. First you must remove East's exit card by drawing the last trump yourself. Then lead a diamond to the queen to put East on the spot.

On winning the trick East will find himself with no good card to lead. A diamond return will let you make a diamond trick, while a spade return will enable you to establish a third trick in that suit. Either way you will have your ten tricks.

FULL HAND

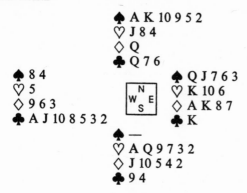

```
                      ♠ A K 10 9 5 2
                      ♡ J 8 4
                      ◇ Q
                      ♣ Q 7 6
   ♠ 8 4                            ♠ Q J 7 6 3
   ♡ 5                N            ♡ K 10 6
   ◇ 9 6 3        W        E       ◇ A K 8 7
   ♣ A J 10 8 5 3 2    S            ♣ K
                      ♠ —
                      ♡ A Q 9 7 3 2
                      ◇ J 10 5 4 2
                      ♣ 9 4
```

RESULT

Your team-mate in the East seat performed heroically on this board. Again West opened three clubs and North overcalled three spades, but East made a far-sighted pass. South was reluctant to bid in case his side got into trouble, and three spades was the final contract.

North and South were already in trouble, for East followed up his prudent bidding with some sparkling defence. After holding the first trick with the king of clubs he switched to the king of hearts! There was then no way for the declarer to avoid a four-trick defeat.

That was 400 points to your team, so you gain 5 i.m.p. for going one off in four hearts doubled and you gain 15 i.m.p. if you made your contract.

Board 45

PROBLEM

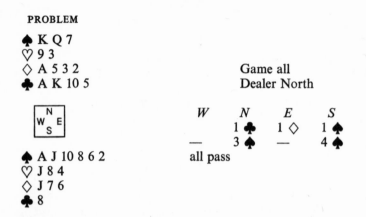

♠ K Q 7
♡ 9 3
♢ A 5 3 2
♣ A K 10 5

Game all
Dealer North

♠ A J 10 8 6 2
♡ J 8 4
♢ J 7 6
♣ 8

W	N	E	S
	1 ♣	1 ♢	1 ♠
—	3 ♣	—	4 ♠
all pass			

West leads the four of diamonds and you win the first trick with the ace. The play of the ace and king of clubs enables you to discard a losing diamond from hand. How should you continue?

SOLUTION

There are nine top tricks and a heart ruff in dummy should provide a tenth. You cannot afford to test the trumps before playing hearts, for the defenders might then be able to remove all dummy's trumps, leaving you with no way of disposing of your third heart.

You will also have to be careful not to permit a trump promotion by the defenders. If East can gain the lead twice in hearts he will presumably lead diamonds each time and you will have to ruff high in hand. That will give West, who is marked with a singleton diamond, the opportunity of discarding a couple of clubs. When you eventually ruff the third heart in dummy you can continue by cashing the king and queen of spades. If East began with a small singleton spade, however, you may then find it impossible to prevent West from taking the setting trick with the nine of spades.

This is really just a matter of proper timing. You need at some stage to ruff a club in hand with the eight of spades, and the right time to do so is at trick four, before West has had the chance to discard any clubs on the diamonds. After ruffing a club you can simply lead a heart and play on cross-ruff lines.

FULL HAND

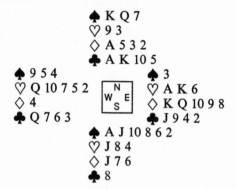

```
                    ♠ K Q 7
                    ♡ 9 3
                    ◇ A 5 3 2
                    ♣ A K 10 5
    ♠ 9 5 4                        ♠ 3
    ♡ Q 10 7 5 2    N            ♡ A K 6
    ◇ 4            W   E          ◇ K Q 10 9 8
    ♣ Q 7 6 3       S            ♣ J 9 4 2
                    ♠ A J 10 8 6 2
                    ♡ J 8 4
                    ◇ J 7 6
                    ♣ 8
```

Note that the contract goes down if you lead a heart at trick four.

RESULT

In the other room the contract was also four spades. The play to the first few tricks was the same and the declarer made no mistake, ruffing a club at an early stage to make sure of ten tricks.

Making the contract therefore gives you a flat board. It costs 12 i.m.p. if you went down.

Board 46

PROBLEM

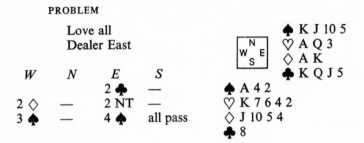

Love all
Dealer East

				♠ K J 10 5
W	N	E	S	♡ A Q 3
		2 ♣	—	◇ A K
2 ◇	—	2 NT	—	♣ K Q J 5
3 ♠	—	4 ♠	all pass	

♠ A 4 2
♡ K 7 6 4 2
◇ J 10 5 4
♣ 8

North leads the nine of hearts. The three is played from dummy, you win with the king and West plays the ten. Which card do you play at trick two?

SOLUTION

The strength of dummy makes it clear that the contract cannot be defeated unless partner has the ace of clubs. If he has that card, a club ruff will provide the fourth defensive trick.

Should you then do the obvious thing by returning your club at trick two? That would be all right if you were facing a robot, who would automatically take the ace of clubs and return the suit. But partner is a thinking animal, capable of working out that you need to have the ace of spades if the contract is to be defeated. He is likely to place you with a doubleton club and hold up, expecting you to win the first trump and lead your second club to his ace.

Will it make the position any clearer if you continue hearts or switch to diamonds at trick two? Not really, for when you win the ace of trumps and lead your club, partner will still be in doubt as to your distribution. He may well try to give you a ruff in hearts or diamonds instead of in clubs.

The way to clarify the situation for partner is very simple once you think of it. Just cash the ace of trumps at trick two. Then partner will know beyond a shadow of a doubt what is required of him when you switch to the club at trick three. He will take his ace and return the suit at something akin to the speed of light.

FULL HAND

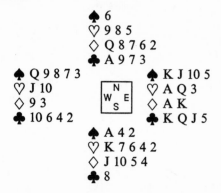

```
                    ♠ 6
                    ♡ 9 8 5
                    ◇ Q 8 7 6 2
                    ♣ A 9 7 3
    ♠ Q 9 8 7 3                    ♠ K J 10 5
    ♡ J 10           N             ♡ A Q 3
    ◇ 9 3         W     E          ◇ A K
    ♣ 10 6 4 2       S             ♣ K Q J 5
                    ♠ A 4 2
                    ♡ K 7 6 4 2
                    ◇ J 10 5 4
                    ♣ 8
```

If you fail to cash the ace of spades before leading your club, you must accept the blame when partner holds off.

RESULT

The contract was the same in the other room, but the opening lead was a diamond. After cashing the ace and king of diamonds declarer led a trump from the table. South went straight up with the ace and led his club, and North had no option but to play his partner for a singleton. South ruffed the second club and exited with his last trump, and the defence still had to score a heart trick for one off.

Cashing the ace of spades at trick two therefore earns you a flat board. You lose 10 i.m.p. if you did anything else.

Board 47

PROBLEM

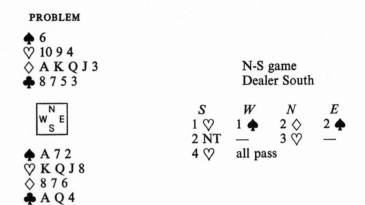

♠ 6
♡ 10 9 4
◇ A K Q J 3
♣ 8 7 5 3

N-S game
Dealer South

♠ A 7 2
♡ K Q J 8
◇ 8 7 6
♣ A Q 4

S	W	N	E
1 ♡	1 ♠	2 ◇	2 ♠
2 NT	—	3 ♡	—
4 ♡	all pass		

West leads the king of spades on which East plays the five. How do you plan the play?

SOLUTION

This looks like a reasonable contract. If everything goes well you might even make twelve tricks. However, there is always some danger of losing control when you play in a 4–3 trump fit. Suppose that you take the ace of spades and play on trumps. The ace may be held up until the third round, and you will be in trouble if the trumps are 4–2. The defenders will cash two spades and force you with a further spade lead, and you will end up with no more than eight or nine tricks.

Nor can you be sure of making the contract if you play to ruff two spades in dummy. That line requires both the club finesse and a 3–2 diamond break for success.

The way to give yourself the best chance on this hand is to retain control of the spade suit by allowing the defenders to win the first trick. The contract will then be safe provided that the trumps are no worse than 4–2. You can ruff a spade continuation in dummy and knock out the ace of trumps. Even if the defenders are able to engineer a diamond ruff, you should still be safe for ten tricks.

FULL HAND

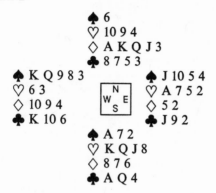

```
              ♠ 6
              ♡ 10 9 4
              ◇ A K Q J 3
              ♣ 8 7 5 3
♠ K Q 9 8 3              ♠ J 10 5 4
♡ 6 3          N         ♡ A 7 5 2
◇ 10 9 4    W   E        ◇ 5 2
♣ K 10 6       S         ♣ J 9 2
              ♠ A 7 2
              ♡ K Q J 8
              ◇ 8 7 6
              ♣ A Q 4
```

RESULT

In the other room South landed in the inferior contract of three no trumps. On a spade lead this had no chance, and your team-mates picked up 100 points.

Playing a low spade from hand to the first trick therefore earns you 12 i.m.p. It is a flat board if you won the first trick.

Board 48

PROBLEM

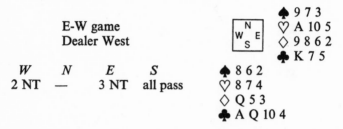

E-W game
Dealer West

♠ 9 7 3
♡ A 10 5
◇ 9 8 6 2
♣ K 7 5

W	N	E	S
2 NT	—	3 NT	all pass

♠ 8 6 2
♡ 8 7 4
◇ Q 5 3
♣ A Q 10 4

North leads the three of hearts to the five, seven and king. West leads the two of clubs, North plays the three and dummy the king. You win with the ace and switch to the eight of spades, on which West plays the queen. North wins with the king and returns the four of spades to declarer's ace. West continues with the jack of clubs, on which North discards the two of hearts. How do you play?

SOLUTION

The distribution of the hand is clearly marked by this stage. North began with four spades, five hearts, three diamonds and a club, while West started with three spades, two hearts, three diamonds and five clubs. Furthermore, since West has only eight points in the black suits he must have at least twelve in the reds. He may have either K Q in hearts and A K in diamonds, or K J in hearts and A K J in diamonds.

That jack of diamonds may provide declarer's ninth trick unless you defend with care. Suppose you return a spade, for instance. West will win with the jack and knock out your third club stopper. You may exit with your last club, but West will be able to overtake his remaining heart honour with dummy's ace and take a diamond finesse to land his contract.

To prevent this happening you must cut communications by returning a heart when you are in with the queen of clubs. If partner has the queen of hearts he will not, of course, cover West's jack. And West cannot at this stage afford to overtake with the ace, for that would permit you to take too many tricks when you regain the lead. When you win the third club you will exit passively with your remaining club, and the declarer will eventually have to lead diamonds from his hand.

FULL HAND

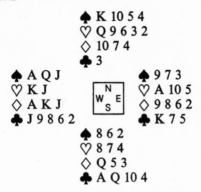

```
              ♠ K 10 5 4
              ♡ Q 9 6 3 2
              ◇ 10 7 4
              ♣ 3
  ♠ A Q J              ♠ 9 7 3
  ♡ K J         N      ♡ A 10 5
  ◇ A K J    W   E     ◇ 9 8 6 2
  ♣ J 9 8 6 2   S      ♣ K 7 5
              ♠ 8 6 2
              ♡ 8 7 4
              ◇ Q 5 3
              ♣ A Q 10 4
```

RESULT

The defenders made no mistake against the same contract in the other room.

It is therefore a flat board if you defeat three no trumps, while you lose 12 i.m.p. if you let it home.

SCORECARD

	Maximum Gain		Maximum Loss		Your Score	
B/F	+ 276	− 13	+ 6	− 266	+	−
Board 41	10			11		
42				12		
43	10					
44	15		5			
45				12		
46				10		
47	12					
48				12		
Total C/F	323	13	11	323		
Net Score	310			312		

By the time you have finished scoring it is almost seven o'clock. You have an hour and a half before the restart at 8.30. Since you are all in need of fresh air and exercise, you decide against dining in the stuffy hotel restaurant with its inevitable slow service.

After a brisk half-mile walk to a local steak-house, a leisurely meal, and a saunter back to the hotel, you feel refreshed and ready for the next set of boards.

SEVENTH SESSION

Boards 49 to 56

PROBLEMS

Board 49

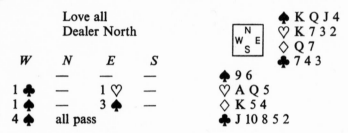

Love all
Dealer North

♠	K Q J 4
♥	K 7 3 2
♦	Q 7
♣	7 4 3

W	N	E	S
—	—	—	
1 ♣	—	1 ♡	—
1 ♠	—	3 ♠	—
4 ♠	all pass		

♠	9 6
♥	A Q 5
♦	K 5 4
♣	J 10 8 5 2

North leads the queen of clubs and West wins with the ace. Trumps are drawn with the king, queen and jack, partner following suit while you discard a club. When the four of clubs is led you put in the jack, West plays the six and North discards the two of diamonds. You return the eight of clubs to West's nine, North throwing the three of diamonds. West then leads the ten of hearts to the jack, king and ace. You continue with the queen of hearts on which West plays the six and North the four. What now?

Solution on page 152

Board 50

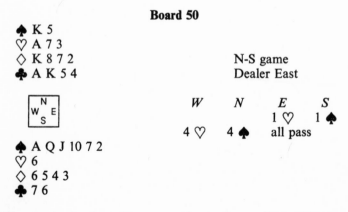

♠	K 5
♥	A 7 3
♦	K 8 7 2
♣	A K 5 4

N-S game
Dealer East

W	N	E	S
		1 ♡	1 ♠
4 ♡	4 ♠	all pass	

♠	A Q J 10 7 2
♥	6
♦	6 5 4 3
♣	7 6

West leads the five of hearts to dummy's ace. How should you continue?

Solution on page 154

Board 51

♠ K J
♡ Q 5
◇ A J 7 2
♣ Q 8 7 5 3

E-W game
Dealer South

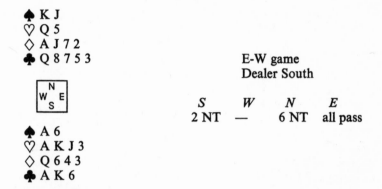

♠ A 6
♡ A K J 3
◇ Q 6 4 3
♣ A K 6

S	W	N	E
2 NT	—	6 NT	all pass

West leads the ten of spades which you win on the table with the king. You test the clubs by playing the ace and king, and East discards a spade on the second round. How should you continue?

Solution on page 156

Board 52

♠ Q 10 4 3
♡ J
◇ K 7 4 2
♣ 10 8 7 5

Game all
Dealer West

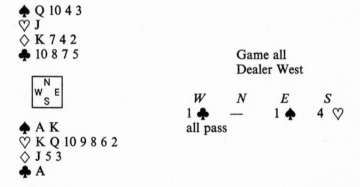

♠ A K
♡ K Q 10 9 8 6 2
◇ J 5 3
♣ A

W	N	E	S
1 ♣	—	1 ♠	4 ♡
all pass			

West leads the king of clubs to your ace. When you lead the king of hearts West plays the ace and East the three. West continues with the queen of clubs on which East discards the two of spades. How do you plan the play?

Solution on page 158

Board 53

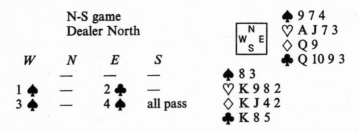

N-S game
Dealer North

```
                                              ♠ 9 7 4
                                              ♡ A J 7 3
                                         N    ◇ Q 9
                                       W   E  ♣ Q 10 9 3
                                         S
 W      N      E      S                ♠ 8 3
 —      —      —                       ♡ K 9 8 2
 1♠     —      2♣     —                ◇ K J 4 2
 3♠     —      4♠     all pass         ♣ K 8 5
```

North leads the three of diamonds which draws the queen, king and ace. West leads the six of clubs, on which North plays the two, dummy the nine and you the king. How should you continue?

Solution on page 160

Board 54

E-W game
Dealer East

```
 ♠ K 9 3
 ♡ 7 4               N        W       N       E       S
 ◇ A J            W     E                     1 NT*    —
 ♣ A Q 10 7 3 2      S        3♣      —       3 ♡      —
                ♠ J 7         4 NT    —       5 ♡      —
                ♡ J 10 9 8 3  5 NT    —       6 ♡      —
                ◇ K 9 7 3     6 NT    all pass
                ♣ 6 4                 *15–17 points
```

On your lead of the jack of hearts North plays the six and East the two. How should you continue?

Solution on page 162

Board 55

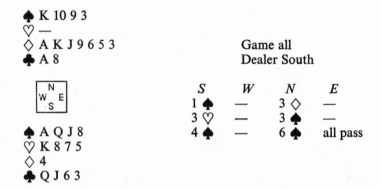

♠ K 10 9 3
♡ —
◇ A K J 9 6 5 3
♣ A 8

Game all
Dealer South

♠ A Q J 8
♡ K 8 7 5
◇ 4
♣ Q J 6 3

S	W	N	E
1 ♠	—	3 ◇	—
3 ♡	—	3 ♠	—
4 ♣	—	6 ♠	all pass

West leads the jack of hearts. How do you plan the play?

Solution on page 164

Board 56

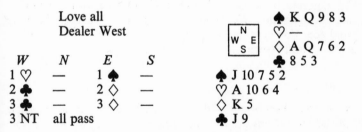

Love all
Dealer West

♠ K Q 9 8 3
♡ —
◇ A Q 7 6 2
♣ 8 5 3

♠ J 10 7 5 2
♡ A 10 6 4
◇ K 5
♣ J 9

W	N	E	S
1 ♡	—	1 ♠	—
2 ♣	—	2 ◇	—
3 ♣	—	3 ◇	—
3 NT	all pass		

North leads the three of diamonds. The two is played from the table and West plays the four under your king. How should you continue?

Solution on page 166

SOLUTIONS AND RESULTS

Board 49

PROBLEM

Love all
Dealer North

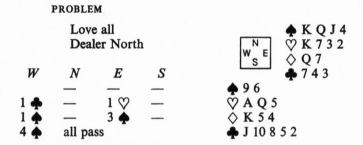

♠ K Q J 4			
♡ K 7 3 2			
◇ Q 7			
♣ 7 4 3			

W	N	E	S
—	—	—	
1 ♣	—	1 ♡	—
1 ♠	—	3 ♠	—
4 ♠	all pass		

♠ 9 6
♡ A Q 5
◇ K 5 4
♣ J 10 8 5 2

North leads the queen of clubs and West wins with the ace. Trumps are drawn with the king, queen and jack, partner following suit while you discard a club. When the four of clubs is led you put in the jack, West plays the six and North discards the two of diamonds. You return the eight of clubs to West's nine, North throwing the three of diamonds. West then leads the ten of hearts to the jack, king and ace. You continue with the queen of hearts on which West plays the six and North the four. What now?

SOLUTION

You know that West began with four cards in each of the black suits, and all the indications are that his other cards are two hearts and three diamonds. The contract appears to be doomed unless these diamonds are as good as A J 10, for declarer has left himself with no way of entering dummy except by ruffing his master club.

A little care is needed on your part, however. Suppose you play a third heart and West ruffs. Your partner has already discarded two diamonds, and when the king of clubs is led at the next trick he will have to discard a third diamond in order to keep his remaining heart. Declarer will then ruff his club in dummy and lead the queen of diamonds, and he will make his contract if he has the ace, jack and any other diamond.

There is no need to put partner's hand through the mincer in this way. Instead of playing your third heart you should return the ten of clubs. The timing is different, for at this stage partner can spare a heart and thus retain his diamonds. West may still ruff in dummy, but he will go down unless he has all three diamond honours.

FULL HAND

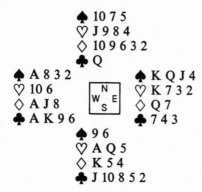

```
                  ♠ 10 7 5
                  ♡ J 9 8 4
                  ◇ 10 9 6 3 2
                  ♣ Q
  ♠ A 8 3 2                    ♠ K Q J 4
  ♡ 10 6          N           ♡ K 7 3 2
  ◇ A J 8       W   E         ◇ Q 7
  ♣ A K 9 6        S           ♣ 7 4 3
                  ♠ 9 6
                  ♡ A Q 5
                  ◇ K 5 4
                  ♣ J 10 8 5 2
```

RESULT

The contract and the opening lead were the same in the other room. Your team-mate in the West seat played more carefully, however, and the defenders had no chance to defeat him. After a spade to the king at trick two, West led the queen of diamonds which was covered by the king and ace. There followed two more rounds of trumps, ending in dummy, then a club was ducked and West had his ten tricks.

You can therefore chalk up 10 i.m.p. if you found the club return to beat the contract. Otherwise it is a flat board.

Board 50

PROBLEM

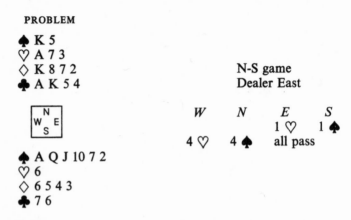

♠ K 5
♡ A 7 3
◇ K 8 7 2
♣ A K 5 4

N-S game
Dealer East

♠ A Q J 10 7 2
♡ 6
◇ 6 5 4 3
♣ 7 6

W	N	E	S
		1 ♡	1 ♠
4 ♡	4 ♠	all pass	

West leads the five of hearts to dummy's ace. How should you continue?

SOLUTION

This looks a good contract. You can count nine top tricks and there are good chances of a tenth in diamonds. The diamond ace is sure to be wrong on the bidding, but as long as the suit breaks 3–2 it will provide a tenth trick.

Are there any snags that may crop up? Well, there is always the possibility that the trumps will break badly. If you draw trumps immediately and a defender shows out on the second round, you will not have time to set up your diamond trick. Four rounds of trumps will leave you with only two—not enough to withstand the heart force each time the defenders gain the lead.

On this hand you need to find the diamonds 3–2, but you do not have to rely on a 3–2 trump break as well. The way to protect yourself is to set up your diamond trick before touching the trumps. Lead a small diamond from the table at trick two. You can ruff the heart return and lead a second diamond, ruff the next heart lead and play a third diamond. If the defenders lead another heart at this point you will be able to discard your fourth diamond and ruff in dummy. On any other return you will be able to draw trumps and make your established diamond.

FULL HAND

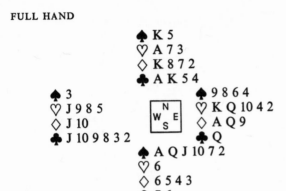

```
                    ♠ K 5
                    ♡ A 7 3
                    ◇ K 8 7 2
                    ♣ A K 5 4
     ♠ 3                          ♠ 9 8 6 4
     ♡ J 9 8 5          N         ♡ K Q 10 4 2
     ◇ J 10          W     E      ◇ A Q 9
     ♣ J 10 9 8 3 2      S        ♣ Q
                    ♠ A Q J 10 7 2
                    ♡ 6
                    ◇ 6 5 4 3
                    ♣ 7 6
```

Partner did well not to double four hearts, which is unbeatable on any defence.

RESULT

The contract was also four spades in the other room but the declarer was not really tested. West elected to lead the jack of diamonds, and South had an easy ride to ten tricks.

It is therefore a flat board if you led a diamond at trick two. You lose 12 i.m.p. if you drew trumps prematurely.

Board 51

PROBLEM

♠ K J
♡ Q 5
◇ A J 7 2
♣ Q 8 7 5 3

E-W game
Dealer South

```
  N
W   E
  S
```

♠ A 6
♡ A K J 3
◇ Q 6 4 3
♣ A K 6

S	W	N	E
2 NT	—	6 NT	all pass

West leads the ten of spades which you win on the table with the king. You test the clubs by playing the ace and king, and East discards a spade on the second round. How should you continue?

SOLUTION

Once again you are in an excellent contract. It is a bit of a blow to find the clubs 4–1, but there are still good chances in the diamond suit. Even if the finesse is wrong, a 3–2 diamond break will give you enough tricks for the slam. However, it would be a pity to take a losing finesse and subsequently discover that the suit did not break. Is there anything you can do to guard against a 4–1 break in diamonds?

If you give a little thought to the matter you may realize that you can make sure of your contract irrespective of the division of the adverse cards. The safe play is to lead a diamond to the ace and return a low diamond towards your queen.

Suppose, in the first place, that East has four diamonds. If he takes his king on the second round he gives you the three tricks you need in the suit. If he ducks your queen will win, and when West shows out on the second round you can safely revert to clubs, conceding a trick to West and thus establishing your twelfth trick in the suit.

If West has four diamonds his king will capture your queen on the second round, but he will later be subjected to a squeeze in the minor suits. He may attack either the club or the diamond entry in dummy but he cannot knock them both out, and he will feel the pinch when you cash your major suit winners.

FULL HAND

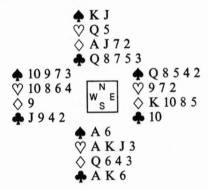

```
                    ♠ K J
                    ♡ Q 5
                    ◇ A J 7 2
                    ♣ Q 8 7 5 3
    ♠ 10 9 7 3                     ♠ Q 8 5 4 2
    ♡ 10 8 6 4      N              ♡ 9 7 2
    ◇ 9           W   E            ◇ K 10 8 5
    ♣ J 9 4 2       S              ♣ 10
                    ♠ A 6
                    ♡ A K J 3
                    ◇ Q 6 4 3
                    ♣ A K 6
```

RESULT

In the other room after a lengthy auction your opponents came to rest in six diamonds. This contract had no chance on the lie of the cards, going one down for a loss of 50 points. Serves the blighters right for playing in such a feeble suit!

Making your slam is therefore worth 14 i.m.p. to your team. It is a flat board if you went one down.

Board 52

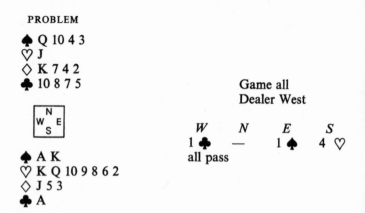

♠ Q 10 4 3
♡ J
◇ K 7 4 2
♣ 10 8 7 5

Game all
Dealer West

♠ A K
♡ K Q 10 9 8 6 2
◇ J 5 3
♣ A

W	N	E	S
1 ♣	—	1 ♠	4 ♡
all pass			

West leads the king of clubs to your ace. When you lead the king of hearts West plays the ace and East the three. West continues with the queen of clubs on which East discards the two of spades. How do you plan the play?

SOLUTION

There are nine top tricks, and the queen of spades is a tenth if only you can reach it. Chances do not look bright. The ace of diamonds is marked in the East hand (what else can he have for his response of one spade?), and you are likely to lose three diamond tricks if you have to tackle the suit yourself.

It would be fine if you could persuade East to lead diamonds for you. To bring that off you must envisage the ending at trick three, ruffing the queen of clubs with the six of hearts, not with the two. Continue by cashing the queen of hearts and, if West shows out, the ten. Then play off the ace and king of spades and exit with the two of trumps. When East wins the trick he will have to lead a diamond or a spade, either of which will give you two tricks in exchange for the one lost by the gambit.

FULL HAND

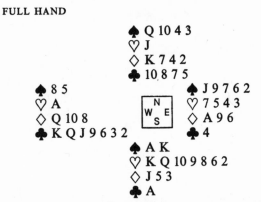

The position is marked when West shows out on the second trump. If he had followed, you would have had to assume that East had the outstanding trump, exiting with the two after cashing the top spades.

Note that if you squander the two of hearts East can escape the end-play by throwing his seven of hearts under the queen or ten.

RESULT

The contract was the same in the other room, as was the play to the first two tricks. West then switched to a spade, however, and the declarer was not severely tested. When West showed out on the second trump the end-play became obvious, and the declarer duly made his contract for a score of 620.

Take a flat board if you preserved the two of hearts, but say goodbye to 12 i.m.p. if you wasted it.

Board 53

PROBLEM

N-S game
Dealer North

	W	N	E	S
	—	—	—
1 ♠	—	2 ♣	—
3 ♠	—	4 ♠	all pass

♠ 9 7 4
♡ A J 7 3
◇ Q 9
♣ Q 10 9 3

♠ 8 3
♡ K 9 8 2
◇ K J 4 2
♣ K 8 5

North leads the three of diamonds which draws the queen, king and ace. West leads the six of clubs, on which North plays the two, dummy the nine and you the king. How should you continue?

SOLUTION

The opening lead marks declarer with three diamonds and on the bidding he must have at least five spades. That leaves him with no more than five cards in hearts and clubs, and it follows that any heart loser he may have will eventually be discarded on dummy's clubs. Clearly there is no time to lose. You must switch at once to a heart in an attempt to establish a trick in the suit.

Do not make the mistake of cashing your jack of diamonds first. Presumably declarer needs to ruff a diamond in dummy, and there is no point in making it easy for him. At this stage you cannot be sure whether the defence will win a trump trick or a second club as the setting trick. You only know that you have nothing to lose and may have a lot to gain by switching to a heart.

FULL HAND

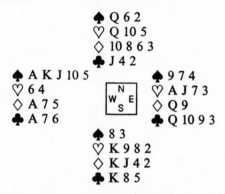

```
                    ♠ Q 6 2
                    ♡ Q 10 5
                    ◇ 10 8 6 3
                    ♣ J 4 2
        ♠ A K J 10 5           ♠ 9 7 4
        ♡ 6 4          N       ♡ A J 7 3
        ◇ A 7 5      W   E     ◇ Q 9
        ♣ A 7 6        S       ♣ Q 10 9 3
                    ♠ 8 3
                    ♡ K 9 8 2
                    ◇ K J 4 2
                    ♣ K 8 5
```

Note that your problems are by no means over when you return a heart to the queen and ace. Presumably declarer will cash the ace and king of spades and continue with three more rounds of clubs, discarding the losing heart from hand. Partner must refuse to ruff this trick, and when declarer continues with the nine of diamonds from the table you must resist the temptation to play the jack. You must allow partner to win so that he may cash the master trump and lead another diamond for the setting trick.

RESULT

The contract and the opening lead were the same in the other room, but when the queen of diamonds was covered by the king declarer played low. It was then even more difficult for South to find the heart switch. In practice he returned a trump, and the extra tempo allowed West to make his contract.

Take 10 i.m.p. for finding the heart switch at trick three. It is a flat board if you led anything else.

Board 54

PROBLEM

E-W game
Dealer East

♠ K 9 3
♡ 7 4
◇ A J
♣ A Q 10 7 3 2

```
        N
      W   E
        S
```

♠ J 7
♡ J 10 9 8 3
◇ K 9 7 3
♣ 6 4

W	N	E	S
		1 NT*	—
3 ♣	—	3 ♡	—
4 NT	—	5 ♡	—
5 NT	—	6 ♡	—
6 NT	all pass		
	*15–17 points		

On your lead of the jack of hearts North plays the six and East the two. How should you continue?

SOLUTION

The bidding has been quite informative, since you know that East has two aces and two kings (was West going to chance seven if his partner had shown three kings?). On reflection, you also know that declarer's fifteenth point is the jack of clubs. It must be so, for if East had any queen he would not have ducked the first trick. He would have won and either taken his twelve top tricks or established his twelfth trick in diamonds.

So East has only eleven tricks and has ducked in order to rectify the count for a squeeze. He has a spade menace against your partner, and if he began with four hearts he has a heart menace against you. Dummy's jack of diamonds will serve as a double menace.

If you continue hearts declarer will cash the ace and king, discarding a spade from dummy, and then run the clubs. On the last club partner will have to bare his queen of diamonds in order to keep a spade stopper. East will then discard his third spade and play the king and ace of spades to squeeze you in the red suits.

The way to break up this squeeze is to attack the double menace. You should therefore switch to a small diamond.

FULL HAND

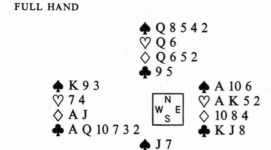

```
                    ♠ Q 8 5 4 2
                    ♡ Q 6
                    ◇ Q 6 5 2
                    ♣ 9 5
    ♠ K 9 3          N          ♠ A 10 6
    ♡ 7 4          W   E        ♡ A K 5 2
    ◇ A J            S          ◇ 10 8 4
    ♣ A Q 10 7 3 2              ♣ K J 8
                    ♠ J 7
                    ♡ J 10 9 8 3
                    ◇ K 9 7 3
                    ♣ 6 4
```

If you found the diamond switch I hope you didn't forget to con-
gratulate your partner on the part he played in defeating the contract.
If he had made the 'automatic' play of unblocking the queen of
hearts at trick one, there would have been no defence when declarer
ducked. The diamonds cannot profitably be attacked from the other
side of the table. If North leads a small diamond he is caught in a
spade-diamond squeeze, while if he leads the queen of diamonds he
exposes you to a red suit squeeze.

RESULT

The same lead was made against the same contract in the other room.
Both defenders were on their toes. North played low, and when the
declarer held off South duly found the diamond switch.

A flat board is therefore the best you can achieve. If you missed
the diamond switch you lose 17 i.m.p.

Board 55

PROBLEM

♠ K 10 9 3
♡ —
♢ A K J 9 6 5 3
♣ A 8

Game all
Dealer South

S	W	N	E
1 ♠	—	3 ♢	—
3 ♡	—	3 ♠	—
4 ♠	—	6 ♠	all pass

♠ A Q J 8
♡ K 8 7 5
♢ 4
♣ Q J 6 3

West leads the jack of hearts. How do you plan the play?

SOLUTION

If everything breaks evenly and the king of clubs is well placed it may be possible to make all thirteen tricks. Your task is to find the safest way of making twelve tricks, however. You will need to ruff diamonds in your own hand, and if the trumps are 4–1 you cannot afford to allow dummy to be forced. You should therefore discard on the jack of hearts and allow East to win the first trick.

There is still scope for carelessness. It looks natural to discard the eight of clubs from the table, but if you do this East will certainly switch to a club at trick two. The removal of the club entry from dummy may be something you cannot afford. If both spades and diamonds prove to be 4–1, you will find yourself short of an entry to establish the diamonds and the contract will go down.

The correct discard from dummy at trick one is a small diamond, for the king of hearts can always take care of the losing club at a later time. Now if East switches to a club you can at least be sure of two club tricks. You can also count on one trick from each of the red suits, and you should be able to score eight trumps on a cross-ruff to bring your total up to twelve.

FULL HAND

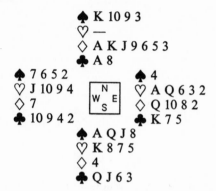

♠ K 10 9 3
♡ —
◇ A K J 9 6 5 3
♣ A 8

♠ 7 6 5 2
♡ J 10 9 4
◇ 7
♣ 10 9 4 2

♠ 4
♡ A Q 6 3 2
◇ Q 10 8 2
♣ K 7 5

♠ A Q J 8
♡ K 8 7 5
◇ 4
♣ Q J 6 3

RESULT

In the other room South opened one club and the spade suit was never mentioned. Eventually North played in five diamonds, a contract in which at first sight there appear to be three losers. However, East found himself thrown in on the third round of trumps and had to yield the eleventh trick either in clubs or in hearts.

Since your opponents scored 600, discarding a small diamond on the lead of the jack of hearts is worth 13 i.m.p. to your team. Any other play results in a loss of 12 i.m.p.

Board 56

PROBLEM

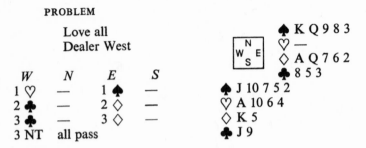

Love all
Dealer West

♠ K Q 9 8 3
♡ —
♢ A Q 7 6 2
♣ 8 5 3

W	N	E	S
1 ♡	—	1 ♠	—
2 ♣	—	2 ◇	—
3 ♣	—	3 ◇	—
3 NT	all pass		

♠ J 10 7 5 2
♡ A 10 6 4
♢ K 5
♣ J 9

North leads the three of diamonds. The two is played from the table and West plays the four under your king. How should you continue?

SOLUTION

It looks as though the defence will need to score some heart tricks to defeat this contract, and it is tempting to switch to a small heart at trick two. The temptation will be easy enough to resist, however, if you reflect upon the bidding. West opened one heart and then bid and rebid clubs, indicating at least ten cards in these two suits. The opening lead further marks him with two cards in diamonds, and he can therefore have no more than one spade.

The hands are a bit of a misfit, in fact, and you can take full advantage of this by returning your diamond at trick two, cutting the last link with dummy before declarer can get the spades going. This will effectively reduce dummy's contribution to two tricks, and it is highly unlikely that declarer can muster seven tricks from his own hand.

FULL HAND

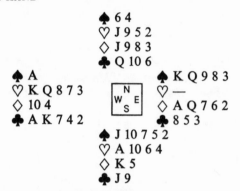

```
                ♠ 6 4
                ♡ J 9 5 2
                ◇ J 9 8 3
                ♣ Q 10 6
♠ A                              ♠ K Q 9 8 3
♡ K Q 8 7 3      N              ♡ —
◇ 10 4         W     E          ◇ A Q 7 6 2
♣ A K 7 4 2      S              ♣ 8 5 3
                ♠ J 10 7 5 2
                ♡ A 10 6 4
                ◇ K 5
                ♣ J 9
```

You can see what happens on a heart switch at trick two. West wins with the king, unblocks the ace of spades, ducks a club and finishes with ten tricks.

The diamond return makes the hand too difficult to manage. The best declarer can do is escape for one down.

RESULT

In the other room the auction started in the same way, but East bid four clubs over his partner's three no trumps. West tried four hearts, East four spades which was doubled, and your team-mates finally came to rest in five clubs.

North doubled and led a diamond, but declarer was able to discard his losing diamond on a spade and ruff two hearts in dummy, making his contract for the loss of one trump and one heart.

That was worth 750, so you gain 13 i.m.p. for continuing diamonds at trick two and 3 i.m.p. for leading anything else.

SCORECARD

B/F	Maximum Gain		Maximum Loss		Your Score	
	+ 323	− 13	+ 11	− 323	+	−
Board 49	10					
50				12		
51	14					
52				12		
53	10					
54				17		
55	13			12		
56	13		3			
Total C/F	383	13	14	376		
Net Score	370			362		

All members of the team are keen to play in the last session, but of course you know what is going to happen even before the captain raises an inquiring eyebrow in your direction. You nod, swallow a couple of aspirins, and step outside for a breath of air.

The time is 9.40 as you stroll back and take your place at the table for the final eight boards.

FINAL SESSION

Boards 57 to 64

PROBLEMS

Board 57

♠ Q 5
♡ A 3
◇ A K Q 10 8 3
♣ A K 9

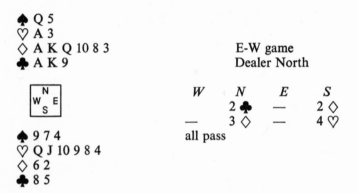

E-W game
Dealer North

♠ 9 7 4
♡ Q J 10 9 8 4
◇ 6 2
♣ 8 5

W	N	E	S
	2 ♣	—	2 ◇
—	3 ◇	—	4 ♡
all pass			

West cashes the ace and king of spades, East following with the jack and the two, and then switches to the six of hearts. You play the three from dummy, East plays the two and you win with the eight. How do you plan your play?

Solution on page 174

Board 58

♠ 10 9 7 2
♡ J 7 4
◇ K J 9 3
♣ 8 3

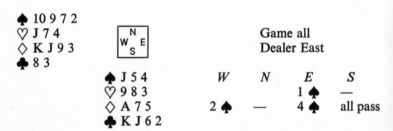

♠ J 5 4
♡ 9 8 3
◇ A 7 5
♣ K J 6 2

Game all
Dealer East

W	N	E	S
		1 ♠	—
2 ♠	—	4 ♠	all pass

When you lead the two of clubs partner agreeably produces the ace. He returns the four of clubs and you capture East's ten with the jack. How should you continue?

Solution on page 176

Board 59

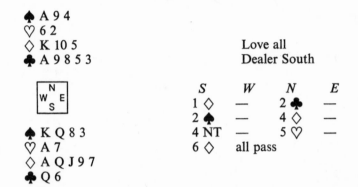

♠ A 9 4
♡ 6 2
◇ K 10 5
♣ A 9 8 5 3

Love all
Dealer South

♠ K Q 8 3
♡ A 7
◇ A Q J 9 7
♣ Q 6

S	W	N	E
1 ◇	—	2 ♣	—
2 ♠	—	4 ◇	—
4 NT	—	5 ♡	—
6 ◇	all pass		

West leads the queen of hearts, East plays the nine and you win with the ace. Both opponents follow suit when you cash the ace and king of diamonds. How should you continue?

Solution on page 178

Board 60

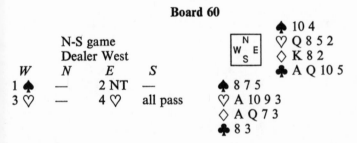

N-S game
Dealer West

♠ 10 4
♡ Q 8 5 2
◇ K 8 2
♣ A Q 10 5

♠ 8 7 5
♡ A 10 9 3
◇ A Q 7 3
♣ 8 3

W	N	E	S
1 ♠	—	2 NT	—
3 ♡	—	4 ♡	all pass

North leads the four of diamonds, the king is played from the table, and West drops the six under your ace. How do you plan your defence?

Solution on page 180

Board 61

♠ K J 5
♡ 7 6 2
◇ A 8 6 3
♣ A Q 5

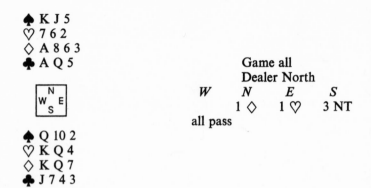

Game all
Dealer North

W	N	E	S
	1 ◇	1 ♡	3 NT
all pass			

♠ Q 10 2
♡ K Q 4
◇ K Q 7
♣ J 7 4 3

West leads the nine of hearts, East covers with the ten and you win with the king. What do you lead at trick two?

Solution on page 182

Board 62

♠ A K Q 10 7 3
♡ 7 5
◇ 8 5 3
♣ 8 2

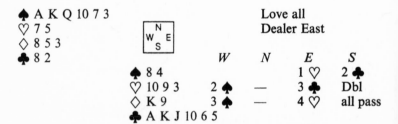

Love all
Dealer East

♠ 8 4
♡ 10 9 3
◇ K 9
♣ A K J 10 6 5

W	N	E	S
		1 ♡	2 ♣
2 ♠	—	3 ♣	Dbl
3 ♠	—	4 ♡	all pass

You start with the ace and king of clubs, partner playing the three and the four and declarer the seven and the queen. How should you continue?

Solution on page 184

Board 63

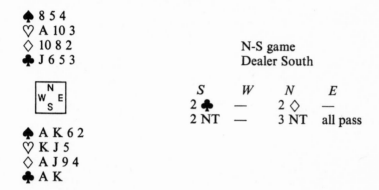

♠ 8 5 4
♡ A 10 3
◇ 10 8 2
♣ J 6 5 3

N-S game
Dealer South

♠ A K 6 2
♡ K J 5
◇ A J 9 4
♣ A K

S	W	N	E
2♣	—	2◇	—
2 NT	—	3 NT	all pass

West leads the ten of clubs. You play low from dummy, East contributes the eight and you win with the king. How should you continue?

Solution on page 186

Board 64

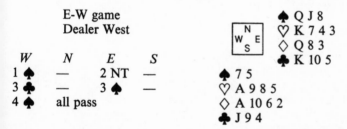

E-W game
Dealer West

♠ Q J 8
♡ K 7 4 3
◇ Q 8 3
♣ K 10 5

♠ 7 5
♡ A 9 8 5
◇ A 10 6 2
♣ J 9 4

W	N	E	S
1♠	—	2 NT	—
3♣	—	3♠	—
4♠	all pass		

North leads the queen of hearts to the king, ace and two. How should you continue?

Solution on page 188

SOLUTIONS AND RESULTS

Board 57

PROBLEM

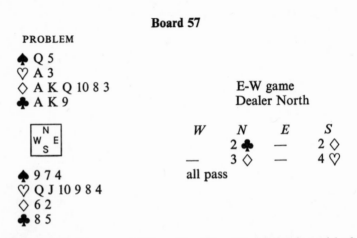

♠ Q 5
♡ A 3
◇ A K Q 10 8 3
♣ A K 9

E-W game
Dealer North

♠ 9 7 4
♡ Q J 10 9 8 4
◇ 6 2
♣ 8 5

W	N	E	S
	2 ♣	—	2 ◇
—	3 ◇	—	4 ♡
all pass			

West cashes the ace and king of spades, East following with the jack and the two, and then switches to the six of hearts. You play the three from dummy, East plays the two and you win with the eight. How do you plan your play?

SOLUTION

You have to budget for losing a trick to the king of trumps, which means that you cannot afford to lose a third spade trick. If both red suits were to break 3–2 you could get rid of your spade loser easily enough by playing a trump to the ace followed by three rounds of diamonds. You cannot rely on such good fortune, however. One or both of the red suits may break 4–1, and it looks as though the safest course must be to ruff your third spade with the ace of trumps.

But there is a hidden danger in this line of play. After ruffing the spade, if you cash the top clubs, re-enter hand with a club ruff and lead the queen of hearts, your contract will still be at risk when the defender with the long trumps has a singleton diamond. He will take the king of hearts and return his diamond, leaving you stranded in dummy with no way of avoiding a diamond ruff.

The way to protect yourself against this possibility is to cash one high diamond before returning to hand with the club ruff. A defender with a singleton diamond will then have no means of locking you in dummy.

FULL HAND

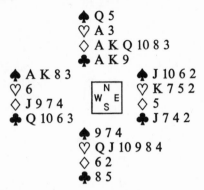

```
                    ♠ Q 5
                    ♡ A 3
                    ◇ A K Q 10 8 3
                    ♣ A K 9
        ♠ A K 8 3                   ♠ J 10 6 2
        ♡ 6            N            ♡ K 7 5 2
        ◇ J 9 7 4    W   E          ◇ 5
        ♣ Q 10 6 3     S            ♣ J 7 4 2
                    ♠ 9 7 4
                    ♡ Q J 10 9 8 4
                    ◇ 6 2
                    ♣ 8 5
```

RESULT

Your team-mates defended well against the same contract in the other room. After cashing the ace of spades, West found the deadly switch to a diamond. When he subsequently gained the lead with the king of spades he was able to give his partner a diamond ruff to put the contract one down.

It is worth 10 i.m.p., therefore, if you took the precaution of cashing a high diamond before ruffing the third club. Otherwise it is a flat board.

Board 58

PROBLEM

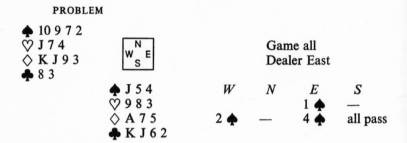

♠ 10 9 7 2
♡ J 7 4
◇ K J 9 3
♣ 8 3

Game all
Dealer East

♠ J 5 4
♡ 9 8 3
◇ A 7 5
♣ K J 6 2

W	N	E	S
		1 ♠	—
2 ♠	—	4 ♠	all pass

When you lead the two of clubs partner agreeably produces the ace. He returns the four of clubs and you capture East's ten with the jack. How should you continue?

SOLUTION

The ace of diamonds will take a third trick for the defence, but what about a fourth? Except in the unlikely event of partner producing a trump honour, the fourth trick will need to come from one of the red suits. The queen of diamonds in partner's hand, for instance, may be all that you need. However, there is no good reason for switching to a low diamond, since declarer's diamond losers can never disappear. Eventually he will have to tackle the suit himself. Furthermore, a diamond switch may be positively harmful to the defence, for if declarer has the queen he will be able to establish discards for losing hearts.

Should you then switch to a heart? The trouble is that you may not be able to establish a heart trick quickly enough. If declarer has a double stopper he may still have time to get a heart loser away on the established diamonds.

The way to neutralize the threat of the diamond suit is by removing an entry from dummy. You can do this quite simply by continuing with the king of clubs at trick three. From partner's return of the four of clubs you know that declarer has a third card in the suit. Make him take his ruff in dummy before he is ready to use the entry.

FULL HAND

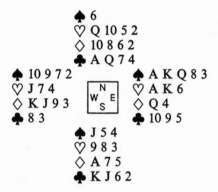

```
              ♠ 6
              ♡ Q 10 5 2
              ◇ 10 8 6 2
              ♣ A Q 7 4
♠ 10 9 7 2              ♠ A K Q 8 3
♡ J 7 4      ┌─────┐   ♡ A K 6
◇ K J 9 3    │ N   │   ◇ Q 4
♣ 8 3        │W   E│   ♣ 10 9 5
             │ S   │
             └─────┘
              ♠ J 5 4
              ♡ 9 8 3
              ◇ A 7 5
              ♣ K J 6 2
```

By forcing dummy with a third round of clubs you restrict declarer to one diamond trick. When the queen of diamonds is led you hold up, and partner's eight tells you to take your ace on the second round.

RESULT

Against the same contract in the other room South chose the 'safe' lead of the nine of hearts. After drawing trumps declarer led the queen of diamonds and was assured of ten tricks whether South won or ducked.

Leading a third round of clubs gains 12 i.m.p. for your team, while anything else results in a flat board.

Board 59

PROBLEM

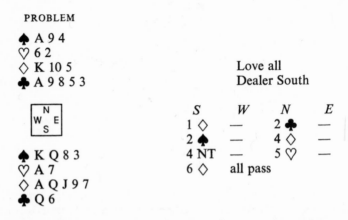

♠ A 9 4
♡ 6 2
◇ K 10 5
♣ A 9 8 5 3

Love all
Dealer South

♠ K Q 8 3
♡ A 7
◇ A Q J 9 7
♣ Q 6

S	W	N	E
1 ◇	—	2 ♣	—
2 ♠	—	4 ◇	—
4 NT	—	5 ♡	—
6 ◇	all pass		

West leads the queen of hearts, East plays the nine and you win with the ace. Both opponents follow suit when you cash the ace and king of diamonds. How should you continue?

SOLUTION

On any other lead the slam would have had good chances, but West has hit you in the weak spot. It is no good playing out winners and hoping to be able to throw in a defender to lead away from the king of clubs. It is clear that either defender can win the second round of hearts, and the one who holds the king of clubs will not be so obliging as to take the trick.

The only chance of making the slam is to try to discard dummy's losing heart on the fourth round of spades and subsequently ruff your heart in dummy. A 3–3 spade break will be of no use to you, for you cannot afford to have an opponent ruff the fourth spade. If you are to succeed you need to find one defender with four spades and the outstanding trump.

If West has the remaining trump you can succeed only if he has four small spades and East the doubleton jack and ten. If East has the trump, you have a choice of plays. You can either play him for both honour cards by taking a deep finesse, or you can play for West to have a doubleton honour. This is just a matter of probabilities. Of the fifteen doubletons West may hold, only six contain no honour card. The odds are therefore three to two in favour of leading the nine of spades to your king, returning the three to the ace, hoping for an honour card to appear from West, and finessing the eight on the third round.

FULL HAND

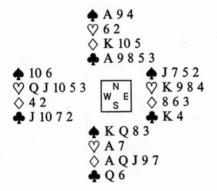

```
                  ♠ A 9 4
                  ♡ 6 2
                  ◇ K 10 5
                  ♣ A 9 8 5 3
   ♠ 10 6                        ♠ J 7 5 2
   ♡ Q J 10 5 3      N           ♡ K 9 8 4
   ◇ 4 2          W     E        ◇ 8 6 3
   ♣ J 10 7 2        S           ♣ K 4
                  ♠ K Q 8 3
                  ♡ A 7
                  ◇ A Q J 9 7
                  ♣ Q 6
```

RESULT

In the other room your opponents were not so ambitious, playing in three no trumps and making eleven tricks for a score of 460.

Making your slam therefore gives you 10 i.m.p., while going down results in a loss of 11.

Board 60

PROBLEM

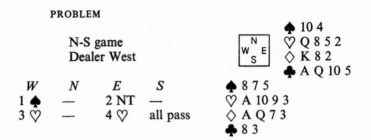

N-S game
Dealer West

♠	10 4		
♡	Q 8 5 2		
◇	K 8 2		
♣	A Q 10 5		

W	N	E	S
1 ♠	—	2 NT	—
3 ♡	—	4 ♡	all pass

♠ 8 7 5
♡ A 10 9 3
◇ A Q 7 3
♣ 8 3

North leads the four of diamonds, the king is played from the table, and West drops the six under your ace. How do you plan your defence?

SOLUTION

Partner's lead of the four tells you that declarer has another diamond, and you expect to defeat the contract with two diamonds and two trumps. It may seem a good idea to continue with the queen and another diamond, forcing declarer to ruff. That will certainly put paid to his chances if he has only four trumps. However, even if the forcing game is the right defence, there is no need for haste. You will always be able to play a third diamond at a later stage when you are in with the ace of hearts.

The danger in playing three rounds of diamonds is that declarer may have five hearts with a 5-5-2-1 shape. In that case, after ruffing the third diamond he will make the safety play of leading a small heart to dummy's queen, learning about the bad break when your partner shows out. On winning with the ace of trumps you will have nothing better to do than switch to spades. West will win, lead his club to the ace, and return the eight of hearts to the nine and jack. A third-round spade ruff will give him a further entry to dummy, and a finesse against your ten of hearts will enable him to claim his contract.

If West has five hearts, you are likely to defeat the contract only if you take out one of dummy's entries before West discovers the trump position. At trick two you should cash the queen of diamonds, and at trick three you should lead a club into the jaws of dummy's tenace. The extra club trick conceded is neither here nor there, for the removal of the club entry practically assures you of two trump tricks.

FULL HAND

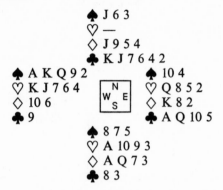

```
                    ♠ J 6 3
                    ♡ —
                    ◇ J 9 5 4
                    ♣ K J 7 6 4 2
    ♠ A K Q 9 2                    ♠ 10 4
    ♡ K J 7 6 4        N           ♡ Q 8 5 2
    ◇ 10 6         W     E         ◇ K 8 2
    ♣ 9               S            ♣ A Q 10 5
                    ♠ 8 7 5
                    ♡ A 10 9 3
                    ◇ A Q 7 3
                    ♣ 8 3
```

RESULT

Against the same contract in the other room the defence began with three rounds of diamonds, and your team-mate in the West seat brought home the game by careful play.

That represents a gain of 10 i.m.p. for switching to a club at trick three. Anything else gives you a flat board.

Board 61

PROBLEM

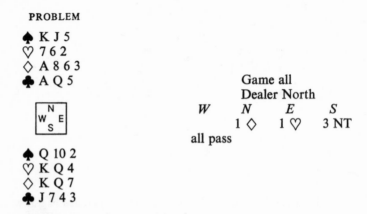

♠ K J 5
♡ 7 6 2
◇ A 8 6 3
♣ A Q 5

Game all
Dealer North

W	N	E	S
	1 ◇	1 ♡	3 NT

all pass

♠ Q 10 2
♡ K Q 4
◇ K Q 7
♣ J 7 4 3

West leads the nine of hearts, East covers with the ten and you win with the king. What do you lead at trick two?

SOLUTION

Nine tricks may not be easy in spite of your combined total of 27 high-card points. If the diamonds fail to break 3–3, you will need two tricks from clubs as well as two from spades in order to make your contract.

If West has one of the key cards—the ace of spades or the king of clubs—the contract is safe provided that you tackle the suits in the right order. It would be a mistake to lead a spade at trick two, for instance, since West might win and lead a second heart allowing East to clear the suit. A losing club finesse would then result in defeat.

Taking the club finesse first gives you a better chance. If the finesse wins you can switch to spades, while if the finesse loses it may use up East's only entry for the long hearts.

However, it would be a mistake to lead a club at trick two, since East may have both the ace of spades and the king of clubs. To retain all your chances you should test the diamonds first.

The correct move at trick two is to lead a diamond to the ace and then cash the king and queen. If the suit proves to be 3–3 you can make sure of nine tricks by switching to spades. If a defender shows out on the second or third round of diamonds, however, you can take your best chance by finessing the queen of clubs.

FULL HAND

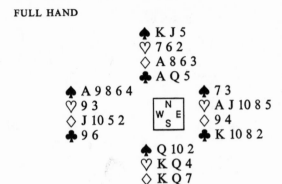

```
              ♠ K J 5
              ♡ 7 6 2
              ◇ A 8 6 3
              ♣ A Q 5
♠ A 9 8 6 4              ♠ 7 3
♡ 9 3          N        ♡ A J 10 8 5
◇ J 10 5 2   W   E      ◇ 9 4
♣ 9 6          S        ♣ K 10 8 2
              ♠ Q 10 2
              ♡ K Q 4
              ◇ K Q 7
              ♣ J 7 4 3
```

RESULT

In the other room your team-mate in the East seat did not venture to make a vulnerable overcall. West led a spade against three no trumps and declarer had no difficulty in making nine tricks.

You therefore achieve a flat board if you attacked clubs before spades, but you hardly deserve it unless you tested the diamonds first. The lead of a spade at trick two results in a loss of 12 i.m.p.

Board 62

PROBLEM

♠ A K Q 10 7 3   Love all
♡ 7 5   Dealer East
◇ 8 5 3
♣ 8 2   *W   N   E   S*

♠ 8 4   1 ♡   2 ♣
♡ 10 9 3   2 ♠   —   3 ♣   Dbl
◇ K 9   3 ♠   —   4 ♡   all pass
♣ A K J 10 6 5

You start with the ace and king of clubs, partner playing the three
and the four and declarer the seven and the queen. How should you
continue?

SOLUTION

It would be very satisfying to switch to the king of diamonds, continue with the nine to partner's ace, and ruff the third round of
diamonds to put the contract two down. But that sort of happy
ending is reserved for fairy tales. Here declarer is marked with a
strong hand. His bid of three clubs was a try for three no trumps,
and you should expect him to have something like six good hearts
and the ace of diamonds. That gives him seven winners in his own
hand, and three spades will bring his tally up to ten tricks.

That does not mean there is no hope of defeating the contract. It
depends entirely on declarer's spade holding. If he has a doubleton
spade there is nothing to be done, but if he has a singleton you can
prevent him from enjoying more than two tricks in the suit by
switching to a spade at trick three. The spade switch will take out
dummy's entry before declarer is ready to use it, and the contract
will go down unless East can establish a second trick in diamonds.

FULL HAND

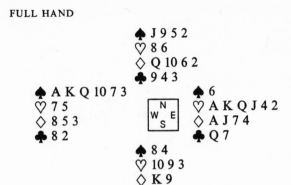

♠ J 9 5 2
♡ 8 6
◇ Q 10 6 2
♣ 9 4 3

♠ A K Q 10 7 3   ♠ 6
♡ 7 5   ♡ A K Q J 4 2
◇ 8 5 3   ◇ A J 7 4
♣ 8 2   ♣ Q 7

♠ 8 4
♡ 10 9 3
◇ K 9
♣ A K J 10 6 5

On the actual lie of the cards the spade switch leaves East with no way of making a tenth trick.

RESULT

South defended correctly against the same contract in the other room. You therefore needed to find the spade switch to tie the board.

A switch to a trump or to the nine of diamonds costs you 10 i.m.p., while the lead of a third club or the king of diamonds costs 11.

Board 63

PROBLEM

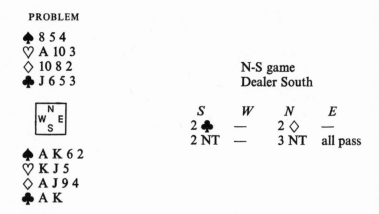

♠ 8 5 4
♡ A 10 3
◇ 10 8 2
♣ J 6 5 3

N-S game
Dealer South

♠ A K 6 2
♡ K J 5
◇ A J 9 4
♣ A K

S	W	N	E
2 ♣	—	2 ◇	—
2 NT	—	3 NT	all pass

West leads the ten of clubs. You play low from dummy, East contributes the eight and you win with the king. How should you continue?

SOLUTION

There are seven top tricks, and at least one extra trick can be developed in diamonds. If you have to lead diamonds from your hand, of course, you will probably lose two tricks in the suit and your contract will eventually depend on a correct guess in hearts. It would be better if you could manoeuvre to lead diamonds twice from dummy, for then you could expect to lose only one trick in the suit.

The trouble is that there is only one sure entry in dummy. A second entry might be found by leading the five of hearts at trick two and inserting the ten, but if you lost to the queen your chances would be dismal.

There is a much better play that offers a seven-to-one chance of success. At trick two you should lead the jack of hearts and run it if West plays low. If the jack holds the trick you can make certain of your contract by switching to diamonds, playing the ace and another. If the jack loses to the queen, you will have in the ace and ten of hearts the two entries you need to take the double finesse in diamonds. After winning the club return, lead the five of hearts to the ten and run the eight of diamonds. If West wins he may be able to give his partner two club tricks but on regaining the lead you can cross to the ace of hearts and lead the ten of diamonds with good prospects of success.

FULL HAND

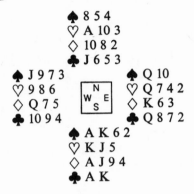

```
                 ♠ 8 5 4
                 ♡ A 10 3
                 ◇ 10 8 2
                 ♣ J 6 5 3
  ♠ J 9 7 3                   ♠ Q 10
  ♡ 9 8 6       N             ♡ Q 7 4 2
  ◇ Q 7 5    W     E          ◇ K 6 3
  ♣ 10 9 4      S             ♣ Q 8 7 2
                 ♠ A K 6 2
                 ♡ K J 5
                 ◇ A J 9 4
                 ♣ A K
```

RESULT

Against the same contract in the other room your team-mate in the West seat chose the unfortunate opening lead of the nine of hearts. With three heart tricks in the bag, declarer had no difficulty in establishing his ninth trick in diamonds.

You achieve a flat board if you led the jack of hearts at trick two. If you led a diamond from hand, you must assume that you would subsequently misguess the hearts and accept a loss of 12 i.m.p.

Board 64

E-W game
Dealer West

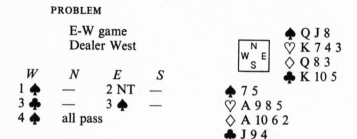

W	*N*	*E*	*S*
1 ♠	—	2 NT	—
3 ♣	—	3 ♠	—
4 ♠	all pass		

♠ Q J 8
♡ K 7 4 3
◇ Q 8 3
♣ K 10 5

♠ 7 5
♡ A 9 8 5
◇ A 10 6 2
♣ J 9 4

North leads the queen of hearts to the king, ace and two. How should you continue?

You can see two defensive tricks, but it is not immediately clear where you may find two more. The obvious defence is to continue with a second heart with a view to clarifying the position and discovering how many tricks you need from the other suits. This is a temptation that should be resisted, however. There is no urgent need for a heart continuation, for if declarer has a second heart loser he can have no means of getting rid of it.

On the bidding, declarer is sure to have a singleton somewhere in his hand and it is likely to be in hearts. The danger of a heart continuation is that it may help declarer on his way towards a dummy reversal, enabling him to gain an extra trick by ruffing three hearts in his hand.

Clearly a switch to either of the minor suits could also cost a trick. This is an occasion for passive defence. You should switch to a trump at trick two, leaving West to do his own work.

FULL HAND

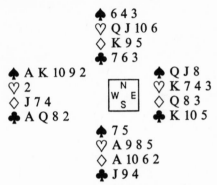

```
                    ♠ 6 4 3
                    ♡ Q J 10 6
                    ◇ K 9 5
                    ♣ 7 6 3
    ♠ A K 10 9 2              ♠ Q J 8
    ♡ 2          ┌─────────┐  ♡ K 7 4 3
    ◇ J 7 4      │   N     │  ◇ Q 8 3
    ♣ A Q 8 2    │ W   E   │  ♣ K 10 5
                 │   S     │
                 └─────────┘
                    ♠ 7 5
                    ♡ A 9 8 5
                    ◇ A 10 6 2
                    ♣ J 9 4
```

As you can see, on a heart continuation (or a club switch) declarer has enough entries in dummy to ruff out all the hearts. He scores three heart ruffs, three trumps in dummy, and four clubs for a total of ten tricks.

RESULT

In the other room the first round of bidding was the same, but West decided that nine tricks might be easier than ten and raised to three no trumps.

When South found the diamond lead the defence could have taken the first six tricks. North should have realized that he had to play for his partner to have both red aces. But match fatigue had set in, and when a low diamond was played from dummy North inserted the nine, allowing East to scamper home with ten tricks.

You therefore earn 12 i.m.p. for your team if you switched to a trump at trick two. Anything else ties the board.

SCORECARD

B/F	Maximum Gain +	−	Maximum Loss +	−	Your Score +	−
	383	13	14	376		
Board 57	10					
58	12					
59	10			11		
60	10					
61				12		
62				11		
63				12		
64	12					
Total	347	13	14	422		
Final Net Score	424		408			

It is 10.45 at the end of a hard day, and I hope that you are celebrating victory by drinking champagne from the cup.

To win the match you needed to come up with the right answers to about half of the problems. If you did better you will have won by a handsome margin. Make sure that the reporters get your initials right for the morning papers.

There is no reason to feel discouraged if you have lost, for many of the problems were tough ones. There will always be another match.